Secrets of Vastushastra

[handwritten notes:]

(solved)

complete the resistance to being body/mind as a reflection of Myself by Being It.

descent in matter

Currently, a trend is evident wherei...
changes by just referring to a couple of books on Vastushastra w....
follow a typical pattern—quoting some rules in Vastushastra and then presenting some success stories related to this analysis. But since the basic assumptions in formulation of these rules are not clearly defined, there is always a chance that rules may be misinterpreted and the application of these rules may not result in the desired solution. This book departs from this set pattern to analyse the logic behind Vastushastra in a unique manner by not only elucidating Vastushastra principles, but also laying due emphasis on the extensive study that must go into any kind of Vastu analysis.

It seeks convergence between Yogashastra and Vastushastra, Astrology and Vastushastra, Modern Science and Vastushastra, etc. This approach has also been discussed in relation to practical problems. A novel concept of 'Balancing and Dynamic Planning' would prove useful for students in this field to understand the essence of Vastu concepts. It is not advisable to go in for reckless structural alternations in the pursuit of instant material gains. Vastushastra basically aims at peace of mind and a healthy life for the dweller, which requires a multidisciplinary approach while applying those principles.

SECRETS OF VASTUSHASTRA

N.H. SAHASRABUDHE
(M.E. (IISC); F.I.V., Vastuvachaspati)

R.D. MAHATME
(M.Tech)

A Sterling Paperback

STERLING PAPERBACKS
An imprint of
Sterling Publishers (P) Ltd.
L-10, Green Park Extension, New Delhi-110016
Ph.: 6191784, 6191785, 6191023 Fax: 91-11-6190028
E-mail: sterlin.gpvb@axcess.net.in

Secrets of Vastushastra
©1998, N.H. Sahasrabudhe & R.D. Mahatme
ISBN 81 207 2042 3
First Edition January 1998
Reprint January 1998
Reprint August 1998

Published by Sterling Publishers Pvt. Ltd., New Delhi-110016.
Lasertypeset by Queff Computers, New Delhi-110066.
Printed at Prolific Incorporated, New Delhi.
Cover design by Rattan Razdan

ACKNOWLEDGEMENTS

Our deep gratitude and sincere thanks to the following personalities who have enlightened us with their studied views and whose moral support was extremely valuable to us during the preparation of this book.

Dr. R.N.Shukla
Jyotirvid Shri Mudholkar
Shri Yesuaji Khadilkar

and
For their contribution in intellectual development the
Late Shri. D.B. Mahatme
Late Shri Vithal Govind Panhale

PREFACE

Vastushastra is an ancient Indian science dealing with construction technology and techniques for building environment-friendly dwellings which are in harmony with nature, cosmic forces and the universe. *Cosmic forces,* is used as a generalised term. It covers the forces like gravitation, electro-magnetism, the electro-weak force and the strong force which are well defined in modern physics. The mathematical analysis describes the forces in terms of their strengths, long range and short range effects, mechanics, various interactions, and in general tries to understand *how a force acts*, but remains silent on questions like *why four types of forces only,* or *why the individual forces act in a characteristic manner only.* Despite the advent of the Grand Unified Field Theory (GUT), the Quark Theory, the Superstring Theory and a host of other theories including the Theory of Everything (TOE), modern physics has not been successful in unearthing the fundamental source of these forces. Vastushastra goes beyond mathematical description of these forces and studies the nature of these forces in terms of their micro effects on plant and animal life in general, and on human life in particular.

We are living in an era of accelerated scientific and technological progress with its attendant turmoil and turbulence creeping into routine human affairs. The pace of an individual's life is being dictated by the changing social scenario. In the work ethos known as *rat-race,* the spirit of competition and one-upmanship is governing every walk of life and over-shadowing the time-tested values like peace, love, harmony, and universal brotherhood. In an era where most men are following a mechanical life pattern, the real purpose of life is lost in the constant struggle of ambition versus achievements, success versus disappointment, happiness versus sorrow, pleasure versus pain, and a sense of victory versus defeat. These conflicting paths can result in mental depression for some individuals who either choose the illogical path of surrender to the transient cults or try to immerse their miseries in wine, women and sex. In the absence of any will to understand the phenomenon of life, for all practical purposes any well thought-out plan to lead a purposeful life is simply missing. Almost every action or response is immature or premature. Even the design techniques associated with human dwellings are undergoing rapid transition with the guiding principle, "a commercial age requires different architecture from that of a religious age". The mass-housing compulsions of present-day human settlements in cities and towns have resulted in a man losing his individuality and identity in rapidly spreading concrete jungles.

Against this background, the authors are making conscious efforts to rediscover the ancient science of *Vastu-Vidya* in terms of modern scientific principles. A practical approach has been adopted. The conclusions and the definitions follow from the inferences drawn from similarities of concepts in various disciplines like Astrology, Yogashastra, Modern Science and Vastushastra. Ancient edicts can be followed only if these are fully comprehended and certainly not because of the faith in the adage "Old is gold".

In this book, efforts have also been directed towards finding a common link between Yogashastra, Astrology and Vastushastra. Reference has been made to a few couplets from ancient scriptures to establish a link between the thoughts expressed therein and the modern scientific viewpoint. This type of correlation serves its purpose in overcoming the unscientific fear of delving into the past. Faith and intellect are not two poles apart, but in fact are two sides of the same mind. In the all encompassing basic tenets of life, these two can be perceived as bosom-friends, co-existing happily. The science of Vastu appears to be closely linked with God and faith. We have endeavoured to study and explain Vastushastra from a scientific angle. We hope that this attempt will spur others to go deeper in all aspects connected with Vastushastra in order to simplify and explain the concepts in detail.

Let us turn to the following couplet of the great saint poet of Maharashtra, Shri Dyaneshwar:

योग याग विधी येणे नोहे सिद्धी वायाचि उपाधी दंभ धर्म — — श्री ज्ञानेश्वर

"Blindly engaging in Yoga practices and Yagna rituals will not lead one to salvation. On the contrary, it will only be a nuisance to others."

A balanced and studious approach is required for comprehending the finer points of Vastushastra. The endeavour should be taken up with due sincerity and integrity, as faith in the cause is a must for achieving success in any field. Faith only can lead to understanding. As the saying goes, "Home is where the heart is". Human abode is associated with values like love, affection, happiness, and pride which are irrevocably tied with pure thoughts, well-defined actions, and faith in God to transform a house into our own 'home'. Study of Vastushastra requires the same degree of love and devotion that goes into setting up a home.

Lord Shankara made the cremation ground his abode to experience the eternal peace, while Lord Vishnu attained his own peace resting on a snake *(bhujag shayanam api shantakaram)* in the midst of worldly disturbances. So, we can say that Vastushastra is a road leading to happiness, but not the only one.

To trace the origin of Vastushastra is a complicated process as its different versions have been associated with various Vedic scriptures and ancient texts. Rigveda, Yajurveda, Samaveda and Atharvaveda in one form or the other, include commentary on Vastushastra-related topics. The primordial sound and letter ॐ (Aum) has great significance for Vastushastra. In fact, the shape and figure of the letter "Aum" as defined in ancient sciptures is found to have a structure ideal from the Vastushastra point of view. It is said that the cosmos evolved from the primordial sound substratum as a force monosyllabic mantra, the ॐ and that all the objects which we see and feel in this universe are sounds of a particular concentration. The shape, the form is nothing but the resolution of sound. Since Vastushastra must deal with shapes and forms, it could have some correlation with the ॐ form (fig. 1.1).

Fig. 1. : Significance of 'Aum' - Directions and Shape

In Vedic literature, the description of the "Supreme Being" is always associated with ॐ, the primordial sound. In the *Bhagavad Gita*, Lord Krishna describes "Aum" as the *adyakshar* (root) of all *aksharas* (letters), *shabdas* (words) and *naad* (percussion) that pervades the space. The concept of "Aum" can be traced to the Vedic times. But, how the form ॐ evolved itself has remained a matter of academic interest. Study of coins and royal seals indicates that the symbol ॐ had evolved well before the 5th century B.C. Considering the fact that written texts on Vastushastra are available from 6th century A.D. onwards (*Manasara* 10th century A.D., *Mayamatam* 11th century A.D.), it is a matter of conjecture that perhaps the philosophy, the science behind the concept of all pervading primordial sound "Aum", evolved into a science by itself, the Vastushastra.

Town planning norms are observed in the Indus Valley Civilisation as represented by the excavated ancient cities of Mohenjodaro and Harappa. Evidence points to rigid north-south and east-west orientation of streets and lanes. In burial grounds, the dead were placed with their heads pointing to the north and the feet pointing to the south. The people of these civilisations, in the absence of instruments like the magnetic compass, used knowledge of stars and astronomy in determining locations and directions of their dwellings.

But Vastushastra as a distinct and separate scientific concept evolved only after the 6th century A.D. and the basic Vedic concepts *Purush* (man or soul) and *Prakriti* (nature or matter) found expression in *Vastu-Vidya* discipline. Logically elucidated and written texts are traced to *Manasara* (10th century A.D.) and the *Mayamatam* (11th century A.D.) which form the basis of most of the later day books on Vastushastra.

The philosophy underlying the varied fields like Vastushastra, Astrology, Yogashastra and in general, the Hindu way of life, is reflected in the great epic *Savitri* by Sri Aurobindo.

> A hyphen must connect Matter and Mind.
> The Alpha and the Omega in one Sound,
> Then shall the Spirit and Nature be at one,
> Two are the ends of the mysterious plan.
>
> *(Book One, Canto Four)*

> In their uniting law stood up revealed,
> The multiple measures of the uplifting force,
> The lines of the World-Geometer's technique,
> The enchantments that uphold the cosmic web,
> And magic underlying simple shapes.
>
> *(Book Two, Canto Fifteen)*

In modern times, Prof. Albert Einstein gave a new insight to science by establishing the equivalence of mass and energy through his well known formula $E = mc^2$ (E is energy, m is mass and c is velocity of light) which provided the theoretical expression to the enormous energies locked in an atom. This concept on one hand was instrumental in the development of nuclear science and peaceful uses (power generation, nuclear medicine, etc.) of nuclear energy, and on the other hand, it degenerated into a destructive nuclear explosion technology as evidenced by atom bombs, hydrogen bombs, neutron bombs, etc.

Energy and matter play an important role in the evolution of human civilisation. It is important to achieve an equilibrium between energy and matter, the animate and the inanimate, and conformity with the opposing geomagnetic forces. If energy is not counterbalanced by matter and life, the stress conditions will lead to fierce and violent incidents akin to volcanic eruptions. If a graph is drawn indicating energy contours on earth, it is seen that peace and prosperity follow the direction of high potential, with poverty confined to areas of low energy potential. In nature, the tendency is towards equilibrium and harmony between various energy fields and the phenomenon is governed by certain principles.

A smoothly flowing happy life is possible through the balance of energy and matter, and Vastushastra holds the key to it. We will proceed onto the study of Vastushastra, by invoking the cardinal principle common to all religions of the world , "Universal happiness through elimination of all evil".

N.H. Sahasrabudhe
R.D. Mahatme

Ist Fl., Venkatesh Villa, 1202/2A/1
Apte Road, PUNE - 411 005

CONTENTS

1

QUEST FOR THE SCIENCE OF VASTU

The same thrill, the same awe and mystery, come again and again when we look at any problem deeply enough. With more knowledge comes deeper, more wonderful mystery, luring one on to penetrate deeper still. Never concerned that the answer may prove disappointing, but with pleasure and confidence we turn over each new stone to find unimagined strangeness leading on to more wonderful questions and mysteries — certainly a grand adventure

—Richard Feynman

Vastushastra is a science of higher dimension. The concepts therein are based on practical observations, research and development spanning over hundreds of years, and are not derivatives of any speculative teleology. Vastushastra effectively manipulates the web of cosmic energy for the betterment of humankind. Its well defined rules and regulations ensure that houses, abodes, dwellings, buildings, and structures in general are in harmony with the surrounding environment and the entire universe. The dwellings subscribing to Vastushastra are always governed by the philosophy of environment-friendly simple dwellings with simple shapes. While modern architecture specialises in bodily comforts of a dweller and functional effectiveness of a structure, Vastushastra aims at ensuring the health, happiness, prosperity, and well-being of the human being occupying the dwelling, and endows him with a sustained peace and tranquillity of mind.

Knowledge and Science of Vastu
Human life is full of events, both good and bad. However, if the mind functions with equinamity between intellect and nature, then the eternal peace and happiness experienced by the person will not let such good and bad happenings disturb his equilibrium. According to ancient scriptures, the world is a storehouse of mind, movable and immovable objects, the animate and the

inanimate, flora and fauna, etc. All the matter and energy in these entities have an interrelationship with one another, mediated by a web of electromagnetic forces. It is a scientific fact that all events and happenings in this world are reflected in terms of light, sound, oscillations and resonances. In the realm of the human mind, a chaotic wave pattern of this oscillatory energy leads to a sense of insecurity, fear and sorrow. Against this, a sense of happiness, peace and good thoughts can be attributed to harmonious and proportionate combination of these waves.

The creation of a healthy edifice can be achieved by implementing even the apparently insignificant rules pertaining to electromagnetic waves, oscillations, resonances and energy — an underlying principle of Vastushastra.

The description or references to deities, demons, good and evil forces in Vastushastra can be explained in terms of constructive or destructive combinations of the various oscillatory fields. Many concepts in Vastushastra are symbolic in nature and need a deeper analysis for proper comprehension.

Vastushastra can be defined as harmonious, proportionate, and positive interaction of all the matters encompassing human life. Vastushastra offers adequate representation to all the factors governing life to create, in a sense, harmonious and melodious music in human dimension. As described in the *Vedas*, Vastushastra is a confluence of two streams which are *within* and *without*. Analysis and diagnosis apart, artistic viewpoint and aesthetic outlook are essential ingredients of Vastushastra.

The Physical World and the Abstract World
The entire gamut of human life is covered by the two concepts — *the physical world* and *the abstract world*. When we study Vastushastra, these two have to be matched properly and equitably in order to build the best possible dwelling.

a) *Physical* includes the following items:
1. Building materials
2. Construction equipment
3. Time duration for completion of the work
4. Rules to be followed for proper construction
5. The architect
6. The contractor
7. Budgetory estimates
8. Skilled and unskilled labour

b) Under the heading *Abstract,* we encounter the mysterious and the incomprehensible. Many minuscule and apparently minor things are not visible, but can only be felt or experienced. There are numerous fundamental facts and theories encountered in Vastushastra which can be visualised only in terms of symbolism. *Abstract* may include the following topics:

1. Religion, religious practices and traditions.
2. The participation and apparent effect of the five elements —*Prithvi, Akash, Tej, Vayu* , and *Jal*—in human dimension.
3. The eight directions.
4. The geomagnetic and other fields.
5. Frequency spectrum of sound waves and light waves, and their interrelationship.
6. Human mind as influenced by traditional values and beliefs.
7. The ancient charts, diagrams and their interpretation.
8. The science of astrology and influence of planets.

Significance of Words, Signs, Thoughts and Symbols

A thought is represented by numerous words. Words are full of meaning. All of us have experienced it sometime or the other, that wrong interpretation of a word can lead to unwarranted complications.

"Word is not the thing." — *J. Krishnamurti*

Saint-philosopher Gnyaneshwar of Maharashtra describes the profound impact of a word in the couplet :

बिंब जरी बचकेची एवढे
परी प्रकाशा त्रैलोक्य थोकडे
शब्दाची व्याप्ती येणे पाडे
अनुभवावी

— श्री ज्ञानदेव

Even though the sun may appear to be a tiny disk, the light it emits fills the entire universe. Similarly, the powerful and all pervading scope of a minuscule word has but to be experienced.

On an individual level, 'words-signs-symbols and thought' constitute an inspiration and a medium of communication for the human mind. Modern neurobiology and medical science in fact can accurately evaluate or quantify an agitated state of mind through E.E.G. technique.

An energy field is created by cumulative action of thoughts culminated at various levels — individuals, groups, communities, etc. This energy field is associated with human psyche and has continuous influence on it throughout one's life. The Hindus call it dormant or inborn *sanskara* (inculcated learning). The individual belief in the ideological entities, the good and the bad, is linked to collective belief of different minds. Even though attributed to *faith*, which generally is a product of imagination rather than logical conclusions, these concepts derive sustenance from within through the support of majority of the human minds. For the same reason, good or bad omens have a special place in any community. Even the intellectuals are not above their influence. A decisive pattern in mind is created by the belief in a particular omen and carves a niche for itself in the entire human psyche.

It can be seen from the above discussion that believers and even the non-believers willingly or unwillingly fall in line with a popular concept and consider it illogical to go against it. The process follows a set pattern. One individual is convinced that 'South' direction is evil and talks other persons into believing the same. Then the entire community develops faith in this belief and a mind-set is created accordingly. It is quite possible that the whole thing is a figment of imagination and yet, gains in status and authority because of the faith of countless individual minds. The net result is that 'South' direction is treated as jinxed.

Therefore, it is considered prudent not to try things unacceptable to the community at large. The psyche of an individual is closely linked with that of the community. The rightful individual actions generally reflect the common beliefs. Not to swim against the current is one of the better policies for an individual.

Swastik, Omkar, Lotus, Goddess Saraswati, Lord Ganesh, the Elephant (refer to figs. 1.1A, 1.1B, 1.1C for some of the religious symbols as reflected in modern science), are some of the symbols Hindus, which from time immemorial have been associated with divinity. Recent studies in the field of bio-energy indicate that these symbols are associated with definite positive energy levels. These symbols generate an atmosphere of devotion, pleasant feelings, and a sense of well-being. The effectiveness of some of these propitious symbols sometimes weakens as the ugly side of the human mind becomes predominant and starts polluting the atmosphere of devotion and piety. The systematic brainwashing through cable and satellite TV programmes and other glossy media is a pointer to this process. It is no longer a matter of speculation

Fig. 1.1.A : Religious symbols and *sanskara*

Fig. 1.1.B : Symbols used in sacred rituals and religious ceremonies of Tantra-shastras, with various modes of electron cloud.

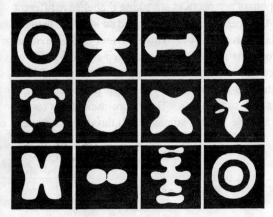

Fig. 1.1.C : Different models of electron cloud in reference to probability density as visualised by Etrwin Schrodinger and reflected in Tantrashastra symbols of Fig. 1.1.B.

that the superficial 'dream-world' projected by these media corrupts the impressionable young minds, as evident in Western countries.

Vastu is a reflection of love and affection between a man and his abode. As such, symbols like *Swastik,* and *Omkar* have their importance for a *Vastu.* From the symbols flows the cultural affinity which in turn creates an atmosphere conducive to proper development of mind. The symbols serve as catalysts in inculcating positive thoughts for all-round development of a child's mind.

Well-known physicist Gary Zukav in his book *The Dancing Wu-Li Masters* comments on the use of symbols:

The function of eastern religions is to allow the mind to escape the confines of the symbolic. Everything is a symbol, not only words and concepts, but also people and things. Beyond the confines of the symbolic lies what is pure awareness, the experience of the 'suchness' of reality. None the less, every eastern religion resorts to the use of symbols to escape the realm of the symbolic.

It has become fashionable these days to proclaim oneself an intellectual non-believer and rationalist by pushing aside the values and cultural-religious beliefs which have been a normal way of life. It is quite possible that this attitude may help in developing a mind with a broad scientific outlook. But a mind devoid of age-old time-tested cultural and religious inputs may act like a robot and may have tendencies towards pre-programmed violence and destruction. By providing proper religious foundation and teaching young children the importance and significance of religious symbols, we can work towards building up a qualitatively superior and responsible generation having all the values of good citizenship.

In this age of micro-miniaturisation in the fields like electronics, computers and medicine, some revolutionary perspectives are taking shape. In a different context, it can be said that "the finer or more miniaturised an idea or a thought is, the more penetrating and effective it can be." The behaviour of an individual is conditioned by the electromagnetic frequencies generated at micro levels of a human brain. Religion can be useful in influencing and controlling these minuscule wave patterns through the sense of well-being projected by the religious symbols, thoughts and suggestions. The micro-oscillations can be linked to the brain (and on a subtle level to human mind) through two routes.

SOUND	LIGHT
/ \	/ \
beat *volume*	*colour* *energy*

In India with each festive or religious occasion are associated certain typical dresses with definite colour combinations. Since many of these events are indicative of seasonal changes, we can infer that the dress combinations are meant for complementing the cosmic oscillations relevant to the time and the season associated with the particular event.

The Hindu practice of sounding of a specific conch on some special occasions underscores the link between human mind and sound energy to suit different circumstances. For religious functions, the conch sound is softly modulated, a different tone announces commencement of a new venture and in a battleground every army had its own distinctive sounding conch — as described in the *Mahabharata*. Shri Krishna, Bheeshma Pitamah, Arjuna, and Karna had their own patent conches. The vibration energy levels created by these conches serve in enhancing the functional efficiency of human body and mind through a type of 'auto-suggestion'.

In Vastushastra, the North-East direction is treated as the direction of 'Heaven', as stress concentration of interacting energies is minimum in this direction. With the same considerations, the South-West is called the direction of "Hell" because of intense energy stresses. The freedom to choose the site, the direction, the size and the entry point in relation to dwelling to be constructed is very limited in crowded townships. But the deficiencies in the Vastu can effectively be tackled by employing symbols, colours, light and sound as prescribed in the Vastushastra. The ill-effects of 'Vastudoshas' can be diluted to a bearable level through this technique.

जे पिंडी तेच ब्रह्मांडी
(Any part of the body reflects the cosmic constitution.)

सोळा सांधे बहात्तर कोठडया
हरिने काया रचिली
नवदरवाजे दहावी खिडकी
आत मूर्ति बैसविली ।।

(God has created the human body as an abode with sixteen joints, seventy-two rooms, nine doors, ten windows and then installed the soul as an image of Himself, i.e., the human body is but a temple.)

As our saints and thinkers have said time and again, "The human body is an abode of God." God lives in human beings and our bodies, the abodes, are in fact, temples. Many philosophers have tried to unravel the link between 'home' and 'God'. As per one school of thought, an imprint of the whole universe can be found in any minute part of the human body. The soul resides in the body and home is where the body resides. The creation of the bodily shape and size, and the existence of the body in a particular environment follow the natural law of selection "survival of the fittest". And yet, the body has its own rules and regulations which at times appear to go against the principles of modern science. The body is an amazing amalgam of *Panch-Maha-Bhutas*, the five basic elements. The science of Vastu also draws its sustenance from these five elements.

In general, it is advisable to construct rooms according to functional activities of various parts of the body. It is noticed that various sections of the house, if planned according to Vastushastra which in turn gives consideration to functions and needs of a body, do not harm an individual's interests in any manner. Vastu can be free from any shackles of dogmas and limitations of unwarranted influence if functional aspect is given its due consideration.

Helix, Asymmetry and Evolution

Man-made things are often symmetrical in shape. But nature prefers asymmetrical forms wherever aspects like preservation and growth are involved. Nature rarely makes a perfectly regular crystal. In the language of crystallography, there is usually at least one *dislocation,* which is a necessary condition for growth at low *supersaturation.* Asymmetry in nature [1] is a catalyst for propogation of life and evolution. Potential difference is the essential condition for energy transformations and current flow. Mathematics can take shape only when the stable 'zero' goes asymmetric through addition or subtraction of the uneven number 'one'.   *1) Sunyata"*

|| एकोहम् बहुस्याम प्रजाजेय ||

"*Ekoham bahusyam prajajeya*", the Vedic thought reflects the concept of asymmetry. In the natural forms, asymmetry of energy [2] always implies evolution of creative life. Vastushastra principles reflect the essence of asymmetry. In fact, it would not be out of place to visualise ancient Vastushastra as a minute replication of nature and energy in a three-dimensional form, using physically available objects.

In Vastushastra, analysis of asymmetry begins with the study of geomagnetic axis. Since geomagnetic flux lines are unidirectional (North-South), the asymmetric effects are evident in other directions. Because the earth's rotational axis is inclined by 22.5 degrees to its plane of revolution around the sun, all the earthly forms are exposed to asymmetry. Asymmetry is also seen in gravitational effect which is a function of interacting masses and distance in-between. The entire nature flows out of asymmetry[3] and all the energy forms, current-flows, and their actions are asymmetric in nature. The key to creative utilisation of this asymmetry lies in nature itself. Helix is the most common naturally available antidote to anomalies and destructive effects resulting from energy imbalances.

In the botanical world, the phenomena of branch formation in trees and ascending movement of a creeper follow a spring-like helical movement. The helix format is observable everywhere in nature — the virus that exists on the borderline of the animate and inanimate, unicellular amoeba, ancient cellular conglomerates, the milkyway have their origin in helical growth patterns. Helix is evident in shells, conches, crustaceans as also in skeletons of many of the now-extinct giant aquatic animals. In the structure of human ear, the spiral cochlear cavity offers protection to hearing organs against intense high-frequency sound waves. The human umbilical cord is a triple-helix of two veins and one artery and invariably coils counter-clockwise.

The yogis visualise the *kundalini* as a spiralling helix, with the vertebrae of the spinal column along which the *kundalini* is said to move and while passing through the six *chakras*, imitate a helical form. The Hindu religious symbol ॐ (*Omkar,* pronounced as "Aum") is an amalgamation of three helices, while the Chinese *Yin-Yang* symbol represents a helix with twin openings. And, the carrier of code of existence, the DNA molecule, is the famous double helix discovered by Watson, Crick and Wilkins.

Yogashastra refers to the *nabhi* (navel) as a *kanda* (bulbous root) and considers it to be the source point of all the *nadis* (channels of energy). The manifestation of energy through the *nadis* is akin to the growth of spiralling helix with multiple openings.

In nature, uniformity is evident in formation or construction of dwellings suitable for a particular species and serving a limited purpose of safety against destructive natural forces. The honeycomb formations of the bees, the conical nests of the termites, the ant-hills, the elaborately woven nest of the weaver-bird, all these shapes are in harmony with nature. The Homo sapiens, gifted with the power of thinking and the ability to imitate nature, learn from nature and project their creativity through construction of material objects.

The history of science demonstrates that success is assured if man incorporates naturally evolving shapes and processes in his designs. Such systems are not only simple, but are excellent from the point of view of energy balance and entropy considerations.[4]

Helix, Golden Ratio and Vastushastra

The flow of energy in the terrestrial atmosphere is influenced by the sun's daily sojourn in the sky, West to East rotation of the earth relative to the sun and the earth's magnetic field. Gravitational waves (yet to be detected in terrestrial laboratories) may also affect the dynamics of energy flow. Helix , a naturally evolved shape, embodies the path of least resistance and balanced interaction encompassing the energy currents of terrestrial, solar and cosmic origin. It is not surprising that the helical form is evident throughout the universe, right from the microscopic virus to the giant Milky Way. As a protective shield, every living oganism shows marked preference for the helical shape. Biochemical energy processes are possible only because of dampening of destructive resonating oscillations through helical structure of certain organs like the pinna of ears.

An astonishing truth emerges if we consider the reality from the Vastushastra point of view. It really is interesting to observe how a Vastu (dwelling) attains a stable helical form just by applying principles of Vastushastra at the planning stage. Considering the directional aspects of geomagnetic field and temperature gradients, it can be inferred that the North-East zone is marked by low temperatures and stable geomagnetic flux lines while the South-West direction represents a zone of maximum temperatures and anomalous magnetic field lines.

The instability accentuates as we move from the North-East to the East to the South-East to the South to the South-West, and then goes on reducing from the West to the North-West to the North to the North-East. This naturally occurring gradation of zones of energy balance and imbalance is utilised by Vastushastra while deciding on the slopes and gradients in a plot. An attempt to rectify directionwise imbalance in geomagnetic field lines and counter-balancing of energy stagnation points through heavy matter results in formation of the famous helix. Constructing the Vastu (house) in the South-West zone of the plot and providing relative rise towards the South-West and downward slope towards the North-East ensures that the helical form attained in the original plot is also activated over the house constructed thereon.

Vastushastra begins the above process by determining the length to width ratio of a rectangular plot and fixing the dimensions of doors and windows in the same proportion. The idea of 'Golden Ratio' (width to length ratio 1:1.618) made popular by modern science and proponents of aesthetics has its origin in Vastushastra.

Vastushastra for the home describes dimensional aspects related to a person's daily routines and energy vibrations suitable for his psyche. *Varnashram*, the Hindu social order based on division of labour and the duties prescribed for a paticular class,is also reflected in the characteristic design and dimensional details of the dwellings suggested by Vastushastra for various social groups. The planning of abodes categorises the designs on the basis of social standing — the king, the prince, the prime minister, the commander, the priest, the teacher,etc.

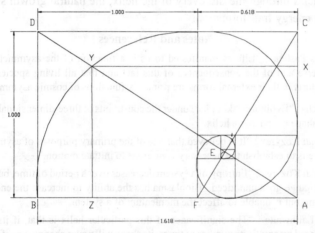

Fig. 1.2 : Helix evolving through a plot having dimensions in 'Golden Ratio'.

Planning of proportionate dimensions of a house based on the Golden Ratio (1:1.618) and using the same fraction for marking the boundaries of the selected plot lead to the formation of a helix (fig. 1.2) with the final microscopic centre of the helix located in the North-East zone, as also positioning of the macro starting point in the same zone. Since the final helix form[5] attained by the Vastu acts in all the three dimensions, it can be considered as an ascending helix for growth and energy sustenance. This type of helical projections[6] result in reinforcing the life-preserving characteristics of the 'Ida' currents[7] in the North-East direction. In a way, Vastushastra provides a naturally energising shield for the human body and mind, that is in tune with the life-propogating properties of double helix of the DNA molecule.

Helix — a Remedy on *Vastudosha*

Deficiencies in an abode, debilitated planets in a horoscopic projection, unhealthy body and afflicted mental make-up are in a way consequences of chaotic energy conditions or interruption to natural energy flow. As such, nature chooses the helix as the smooth growth form for preserving, modulating and directing energy flow so as to bestow bliss on various life forms.

Vastushastra principles makes it possible to attain three-dimensional helix form in every room of the Vastu, the Vastu itself, and the plot through proper landscaping, arrangement of floor levels and gradients, colour schematic and positioning of material objects and things inside a room. By observing nature closely, Vastushastra has bequeathed upon mankind a cure for all ills and deficiencies through the discovery of the helix, the natural growth shape for creative energy transformation.

Notes and References

1. Louis Pasteur : "Life as manifested to us is a function of the asymmetry of the universe and of the consequences of this fact and that all living species in their structure, in their external forms are primarily functions of cosmic asymmetry."

2. Stevens : "Evolution takes place under the constraints of three-dimensional space...- The shape of space is a helix."

3. Nikolai Kozyrev : "It is believed that one of the primary purposes of asymmetry in nature is to establish the necessary conditions to initiate motion."

4. Nikolai Kozyrev : "Entropy of a system decreases over a period of time, but usually this change goes unnoticed. Bioplasma has the ability to increase the energy of a system, but is unable to affect the momentum of a system."

5. Eric Laithwaite : "The significance of this particular helix is that, if its scale is increased by any finite number of times, its shape will never change, i.e., if you look at the tiny central portion of the helix through a microscope, you will appear to be looking at the original helix unchanged. It is, therefore, a natural curve for anything that is required to grow and retain its topological identity. In modern terms, it is a simple 'fractal'."

6. This filament, which some believe to be the DNA-RNA complex, is always in the form of a spiral or a helix, in other words, a coil. Therefore, each cell and its filament may react as a tuned circuit if its resonant frequency can be approximated by an external oscillating source.

7. Refer to the chapter on Yogashastra and Vastushastra.

2

MODERN SCIENCE AND VASTUSHASTRA

In the night of Brahman, Nature is inert, and cannot dance till Shiva wills it : the rapture rises from His dancing and sends through inert matter pushing waves of awakening sound, and lo! matter also dances appearing as a glory round Him. Dancing, He sustains its manifold phenomena. In the fulness of time, still dancing, He destroys all forms and names by fire and gives new rest. This is poetry, but none the less science.

——Ananda Coomaraswamy in 'The Dance of Shiva'

The subject of Vastushastra begins with the study of the earth. This study can reveal the secret mysteries of Vastushastra. Traditionally, this exotic subject shrouded in mysteries has been associated with a language of symbols and signs. We can understand the hidden beauty of these signs, and symbols and correlate the edicts with definite logical principles only through systematic scientific inquiry. We start our exploration in terms of various facts and ground realities pertaining to the earth as a planet in the solar system.

The Planet Earth and Vastushastra
The earth has three different and distinct motions (fig. 2.1):
1. The earth spins like a top (rotation and precession).
2. The earth travels around the sun (orbital motion).
3. The earth moves through the Milky Way along with other planets of the solar system, around the centre of the universe.

The earth spins around its axis, an imaginery line connecting the North and South Poles. Because of this spinning motion, the sun appears to be moving from the East to the West. The earth tilts by about 23.5 degrees with respect to the orbital plane. This tilt and the earth's motion around the sun cause changes of the seasons.

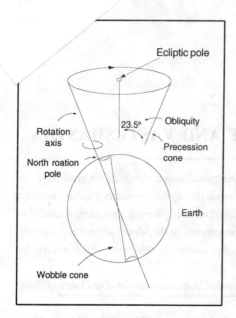

Fig. 2.1 : Sketch of the precession and wobble of the earth's rotation axis. Although shown together in this diagram, the Chandler wobble and the precession are not related. The rotation axis takes 25,800 years to precess once around the cone in space, and 14 months to go around the wobble cone within the earth. The angle of the wobble cone is small, about 0.3 second of the arc.

The spin of the earth may be changed by three distinct physical processes:

1. redistribution of matter on and within the earth (or, in the language of physics, a change in the axial moment of inertia of the earth),

2. an exchange of rotational energy between the earth and the moon (and the sun), and

3. an exchange of rotational energy between the solid and fluid parts of the earth. All these processes act in various combinations to produce observable effects, including the changes in the length of day.

The sun and the earth are bound by a mutually interacting force. This force of attraction known as gravitation, acts on all the bodies in the universe. The force of gravity varies from place to place on the earth. It is stronger at the poles than at the equator, stronger at the sea levels than at the mountain tops. The force of gravitation is of prime importance in the Vastushastra.

We also have to consider the force of magnetism. The magnetism of the earth is similar to the one that is obtained when electricity flows through a coil of wire. The earth's magnetic force is particularly evident in the magnetosphere, a region that is shaped like a doughnut which acts on charged particles like protons and electrons trying to enter the earth's atmosphere from outer space. The magnetic field of the earth is weak, but it provides a shield against cosmic rays. The source of the magnetic field is supposed to be large loops of electric

Water +G → G attracts thru common elements e.g. O₂

current within the earth. The current is generated by a 'self-exciting type dynamo' resulting from circulation of molten rock in the earth's outer core. Because of the close proximity between the magnetic axis and the rotational axis of the earth, some scientists believe that the 'dynamo' draws its energy from the earth's rotation.

Let us now examine whether we can correlate the motion of the earth, the forces of electromagnetism and gravitation and their macroscopic and microscopic effects on human beings and human dwellings.

1) The three motions of the earth lead to interdependent and dynamic interaction between the various active forces (fig. 2.2).

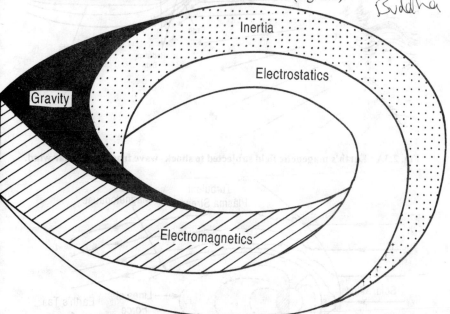

Fig. 2.2 : Interdependent action of various force fields on all the entities on earth leading to a combined interleaved energy envelops.

2) Gravitation and geomagnetism are the two forces which have direct influence on the animate and inanimate objects on this earth. Gravitation is the force of attraction, but the magnetic effect includes the forces of attraction and repulsion. Some physicists are trying to introduce a short range force of repulsion in mathematics of gravitation force equations in Einstein's theory of relativity to achieve a symmetry of the type evident in Maxwell's equations on electromagnetism.

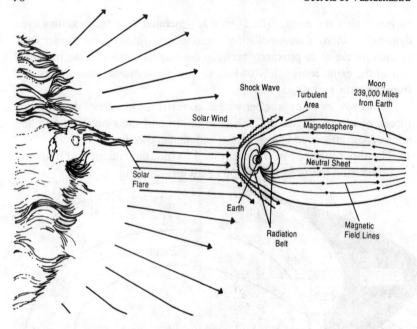

Fig. 2.3A : Earth's magenetic field subjected to shock -wave front from solar wind.

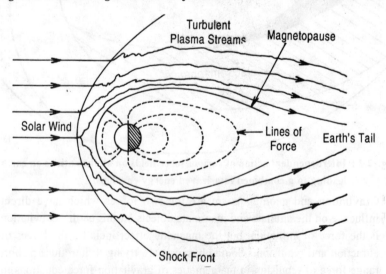

Fig. 2.3B: Conceptual sketch showing the flow of solar plasma around the earth's magnetopause. The earth's magenetic field is distorted into a teardrop-shape by the force of the solar wind.

atom | Human body = earth = universe

A   T   O   M

3) Force of gravitation is represented by exchange of massless particles called *gravitons*. This concept is similar to exchange of massless *photons* in electromagnetism and in general, exchange of 'bosons' associated with various energy-field equations in quantum mechanics.

4) Magnetic force lines emanate from the magnetic North pole and terminate in the South pole (these are imaginery lines along the magnetic field).

5) Inclination of the earth at 23.5 degrees to the horizontal, a strong wind from the East to the West and the spin of the earth create stress concentration in the South-West direction. This direction is also subjected to shock-wave front (figs. 2.3A, 2.3B) when the solar wind is stopped by the earth's magnetosphere or the magnetic shield. Thus the South-West is the most unstable zone.

6) The North-East (direction diagonally opposite to the South-West) remains in a comparatively stable state as regards the solar wind and electromagnetic fluctuations.

7) Elementary cosmic particles enter the earth's magnetic field and travel along the geomagnetic force lines to gather at the polar regions of the earth. The primary charged cosmic particles and the secondary radiation particles create stress concentration at the South and South-West directions. Cosmic rays consist mainly of low energy protons and electrons apart from secondary 'shower' of interaction and resonance particles which may include leptons, hedrons, and massless exchange particles generated when the primary charged particles collide with atmospheric atoms and molecules. Elementary cosmic particles get entangled in distorted networks of force lines in the South and South-West sectors and start resonating at dislocated nodal points, giving rise to hazardous radiations which build up in geometric progression. This creates chaotic energy fields in the South and South-West directions.

8) The earth's magnetic field is represented in terms of lines of force diverging from one pole and converging on the other. A charged particle inducted into this field perpendicular to a line of force goes around it in a circle / with a radius directly proportional to the particle's mass and velocity and inversely proportional to the strength of the magnetic field. Protons are massive compared to electrons and travel in larger circles and in the opposite direction to the electrons. All particles go into closely spaced circles near the geomagnetic poles where the magnetic field is stronger as indicated by the

converging lines of force.| Two-dimensional circles are turned into three-dimensional spirals or helices (fig. 2.4) when particles possess a component of velocity parallel to the line of force in addition to the perpendicular component. A charged particle starting at the geomagnetic equator spirals poleward around its private line of force, tightening the spiral as it travels. On the reverse trip, it loosens the spiral. Sometimes the earth's converging field acts like a magnetic mirror that reflects particles from pole to pole, especially for high energy protons with velocity parallel to the magnetic line of force substantial relative to the total velocity. The radiation effects of the high energy particles are particularly severe in the Western direction.

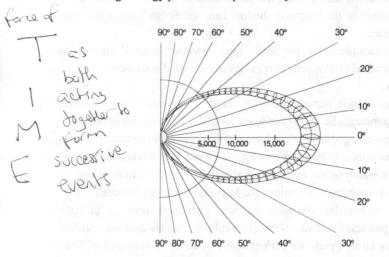

Fig 2.4:   Charged particles trapped in the radiation zones spiral back and forth from pole to pole along magenetic lines of forces. Superimposed upon the spiral they bounce in an East or West drift around the earth, the direction depending upon the sign of the trapped particles. Protons drift East to West and electrons West to East.

9) The other important particle motion is the East-to-West drift of protons and West-to-East drift of electrons that is added to the North-South spirals. This longitudinal drift is caused by the fact that the strength of the earth's magnetic field varies with height and pushes the spiralling/oscillating particles eastwards or westwards depending upon their electrical charge.

10) High temperatures or abnormal variations in temperatures create distortion in the force lines of a magnetic flux, creating a chaos in the energy field.

Traverse of the sun along the East-South-West path (fig. 2.5) creates temperature variations, disturbing the symmetry of magnetic force lines in the South-West region. Once again, a typical imbalance in energy fields is evident in the South and South-West zones, the danger zones in Vastushastra.

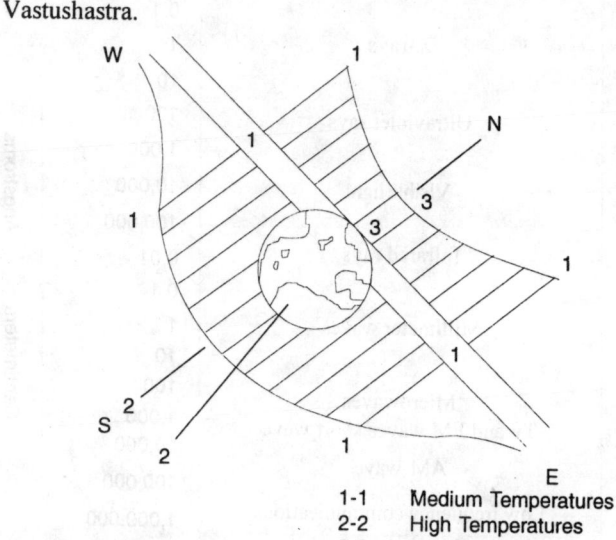

1-1   Medium Temperatures
2-2   High Temperatures
3-3   Low Temperatures

Fig. 2.5 : Temperature differentials with respect to directions due to East-South-West traverse of the sun.

Violet	Blue	Green	Yellow	Orange	Red
4000	5000			6000	7000

Wavelength (Angstroms)

Fig.2.6A : The visible light spectrum ranges between approximately 1,000 and 7,000 angstroms.

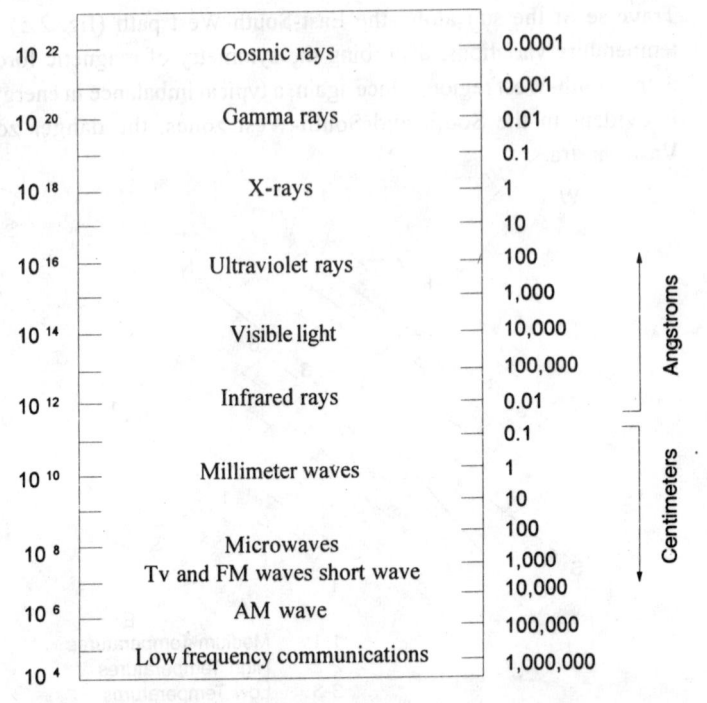

10²²	Cosmic rays	0.0001
		0.001
10²⁰	Gamma rays	0.01
		0.1
10¹⁸	X-rays	1
		10
10¹⁶	Ultraviolet rays	100
		1,000
10¹⁴	Visible light	10,000
		100,000
10¹²	Infrared rays	0.01
		0.1
10¹⁰	Millimeter waves	1
		10
10⁸	Microwaves	100
	Tv and FM waves short wave	1,000
		10,000
10⁶	AM wave	100,000
10⁴	Low frequency communications	1,000,000

Angstroms — Centimeters

Fig. 2.6.B: Visible light region spans a tiny portion of the total electromagnetic spectrum.

11) The sunlight is primarily a visible part of the broad electro-magnetic spectrum (figs. 2.6A, 2.6B) and is represented as oscillating electro magnetic field, with energy transfer mediated by massless exchange particles called 'photons'. When a sunbeam strikes any water surface, the light gets polarised in transverse direction. Polarisation results in uniform amplitude, harmonic vibrations and a beautifully ordered wave pattern (figs. 2.7A, 2.7B, 2.7C, 2.7D).

12) Apart from the daylight radiation, we also have to consider the night-time cosmic radiation. The night sky is filled with waves of electromagnetic radiation. Characteristic infrared and ultraviolet waves are emitted by constellations and are reflected by our own sun to the surface of the moon and back to the earth. The radiating light consists of low intensity hues of red, green, near-infrared, and near-ultraviolet. The human eye is restricted to the narrow visible portion of the electromagnetic spectrum. Though not visible to the ordinary human eye, these night radiations do have a definite effect on our lives and on nature around us.

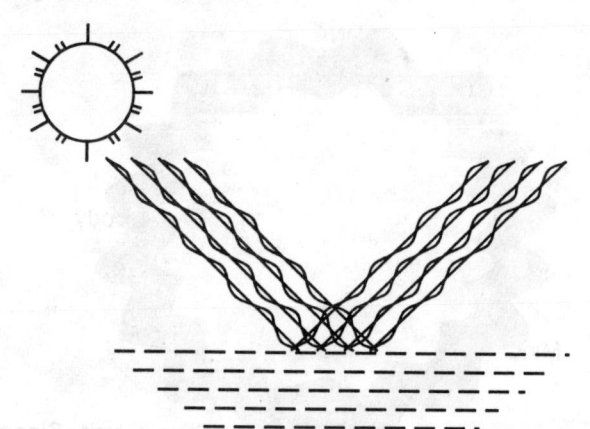

Fig 2.7.A : Sunlight reflected off a water surface is circularly polarised. The early
morning polarised light is beneficial to human body and mind as a
source of energy and vitality.

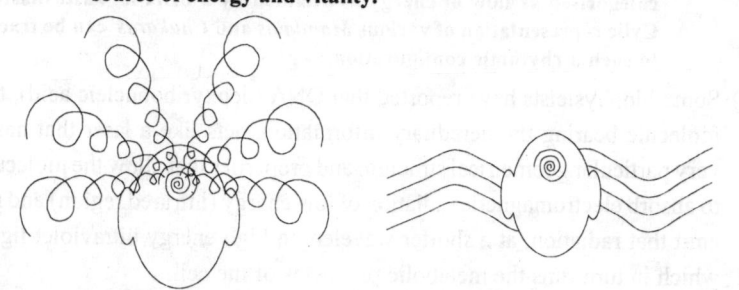

Fig. 2.7.B :The sketch on the left represents EEG wave patterns of a disturbed
brain. The sketch on the right indicates a brain at peace with the
universe reflecting an alpha (X) rhythm, a type of polarised energy
wave.

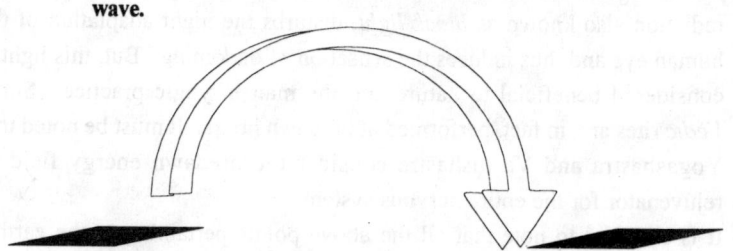

Fig. 2.7.C : Body, mind and intellect attain harmony through polarised energy
field carrier signal called 'Bliss'. Vastushastra tries to create one
unified energy field through amalgamation of all disciplined, ordered
polarised patterns of all the energies. Classically, this is termed as
'Divine Space' (*Divya-sankash*).

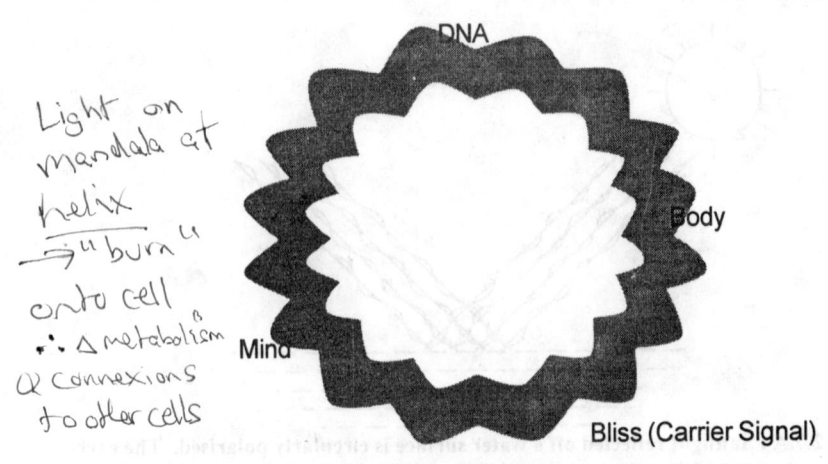

Light on mandala at helix → "burn" onto cell ∴ Δ metabolism & connexions to other cells

Fig. 2.7.D : Rhythmic cyclic representation of the carrier signal 'bliss' can be categorised as flow of energy as attained by a helix in Vastushastra. Cylic representation of various *Mandalas* and *Chakaras* can be traced to such a rhythmic configuration. *Helix*

13) Some biophysicists have reported that DNA (deoxyribonucleic acid), the molecule bearing the hereditary information, acts like a laser that has a very particular geometrical structure and properties that allow the molecule to absorb electromagnetic radiation of low energy (infrared region) and re-emit that radiation, at a shorter wavelength high energy ultraviolet light, which in turn runs the metabolic processes of the cell.

14) The blurred light in the predawn sky is characterised by ultraviolet light (close to the visible portion of the spectrum). The flooding of UV light usually occurs at least an hour before any trace of dawn. This ultraviolet radiation also known as *black light*, disturbs the night adaptation of the human eye and thus induces the sensation of darkening. But, this light is considered beneficial to nature and the man in yogic practice. Some *Vedic* rites are, in fact, performed at predawn hours. It must be noted that Yogashastra and Vastushastra consider the predawn energy field as rejuvenator for the entire nervous system.

It is essential to note that all the above points pertaining to the earth's rotation, gravity, geomagnetism, electromagnetic radiation (visible light, ultraviolet light, infrared light, etc.), solar wind, temperature differentials were thoroughly examined by the seers codifying Vastushastra principles, to arrive at definite solutions for human dwellings in tune with cosmic environment.

angles govern how fast an object moves, where its going & its construction / harmony higher that fill the cosmic space. The cosmic rays have to penetrate a layer of the earth's atmosphere and undergo a complex chain of transmuta before reaching the earth. As such, the radiation reaching the earth (second cosmic radiation) is vastly different from the one existing in the outer spa (primary cosmic radiation). In the vicinity of the earth, the primary cosmi radiation consists of galaxial cosmic radiation by unidentified remote stellar objects and of solar cosmic radiation.

The cosmic radiation in the region of the solar system remains isotropic and constant in time. The particles in primary cosmic rays consist of :

1) protons, deuterons and tritons;
2) alpha particles, nuclei of hellium and their isotopes;
3) light nuclei like lithium, beryllium and boron;
4) medium nuclei like carbon, oxygen, nitrogen, fluorine;
5) heavy nuclei;
6) very heavy nuclei.

In the primary cosmic rays, there is an abundance of protons, alpha-particles and light nuclei compared to other groups. Electron flux constitutes 1.5 per cent of the total flux of cosmic particles with the positrons contributing a negligible 0.3 per cent.

The earth's magnetic field prevents particles with relatively small energies from entering the atmosphere. For example, the minimum momentum a proton must have to enter the atmosphere at the equator is 15 GeV per sec, while at the magnetic pole the same particle can enter the atmosphere with minimum momentum. In general, the intensity of primary cosmic radiation depends on the geomagnetic latitude ('latitude effect'). The earth's magnetic field also prohibits certain directions of entrance of particles into the atmosphere. Positively charged particles cannot enter the atmosphere at certain angles ("Stermer's forbidden cone") to the horizon. It is experimentally found that the intensity of cosmic radiation depends on the orientation of the detector with respect to the points of the compass ('azimuthal effect'). This effect is also known as the 'East-West Asymmetry Effect'. Without going into the mathematics of the process, we can say that it provides the proof that primary cosmic radiation consists of positively charged particles and that maximum flux of particles enters the atmosphere from the 'West' direction.

It really is amazing that Vastushastra also terms the West as one of the evil directions along with the South and the South-West. Vastushastra prescribes certain procedures for avoiding ill effects of deficiencies in the West direction.

A deeper analysis of these practices indicate a definite methodology to offer protection against radiation from the West direction.

Nuclear Science and Vastushastra

In natural conditions man is exposed to cosmic rays and to radioactivity of minerals contained in the earth's crust to a relatively harmless dose of 0.1 rem per year (rem = roentgen equivalent man, a radiation measurement parameter). But in general, nuclear radiation has highly damaging effect on all living matters from viruses to bacteria to mammals. The nature and extent of damage depends on the irradiation dose and on the species of particles. The same radiation has different effects on different organs and on different organisms. The reason why nuclear radiation is considered dangerous is that even high doses are imperceptible to man's senses.

In designing walls for radiation protection, radiation energy and intensity have to be considered as flux of radiation particles decays exponentially with the distance travelled by them in a particular material. To attenuate gamma radiation of 3 MeV energy by 10 times, it requires a 5 cm thick lead (Pb) wall, or 8.5 cm thick iron (Fe) wall or concrete wall 30 cm thick, or water trap 60 cm deep (fig. 2.9). Concrete is generally preferred for radiation protection purposes as it is one of the cheapest materials.

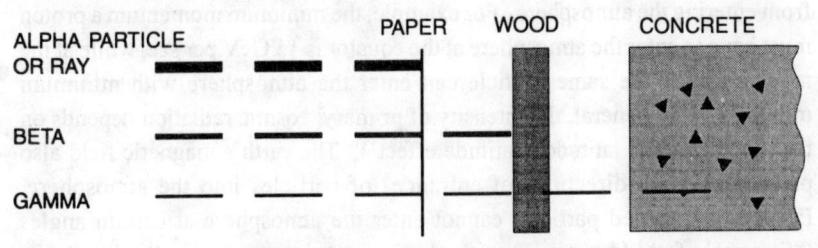

Alpha, beta, and gamma penetrations

Fig. 2.9 : Attenuation of radiation through different types of materials.

The above discussion pertains to high-intensity radiation doses. Vastushastra considers even the minor radiation fluxes while postulating the basic principles for designing an abode for a human being. The essence of Yogashastra and Vastushastra lies in their ability to understand and control the *sukshma* (micro) effects through external factors like solar radiation, electromagnetic radiation, etc., on the smallest of cells or the most difficult to locate nerves in the human body. While Yogashastra trains the body and the mind to live in harmony with nature, Vastushastra creates the requisite harmonic conditions. Compensation of gravitational mass and blocking of the South, the South-West and the West directions as explained in Vastushastra, offer substantial protection to human body against solar, cosmic, and electromagnetic radiation, and the radiation coming from the earth's interior and the crust through its mineral deposits.

Vastushastra Tradition and Scientific Reflections

Every religion of Indian origin looks at life through a well-developed scientific logic. This is apart from the solid foundation of Vedic ancient science that is reflected in every school of thought.

Buddhist literature does not insist on learning new things about reality, but always talks about removing veils of ignorance that stand between a man and his real self.

According to the *Jain* logic of *Syadvad* (*syad* means *maybe*), every fact of reality should be described in seven ways with a combination of affirmation and negation of parameters like existence, non-existence, occurrence, expressibility, inexpressibility, determinateness and indeterminateness.

In *Aristotelian* (or Western) logic, the immediate response is examination of an entity from a particular viewpoint and not from all different viewpoints. The stress is on repeated observations from a fixed standpoint to endow the viewpoint a semblance of objectivity. But the fact is that an object can never be examined from an identical standpoint, as regardless of other unchanged conditions the two instants of observation are inherently different. As the Greek philosopher Heraclitus had put it, "You cannot twice step into the same water" and then Cratylus commenting, "You cannot do that even once." In a sense, nothing is exactly repeatable. On the other hand, *Syadvad* asserts that knowledge of reality is possible only by denying the absolute attitude and stresses on investigating reality from all the possible viewpoints. While interpreting Vastushastra in terms of modern science is a must for further developments in this field, arguments of *Syadvad* can help us in understanding the actual scope of Vastushastra.

Vastushastra and Scientific Analysis

Science can be shared by all men because of its self-evident objectivity and its ability to rise above any kind of dogmatism, personal prejudices or beliefs. *Experience* of any kind is a subjective process. Science manages to convert this subjective experience into objective logical statements through statistical analysis and by the process of comparing pairs of subjective impressions to remove the subjectivity factor. Vastushastra will find universal appeal if efforts are made to scientifically study and understand the subject. Success stories of application of Vastushastra should be evaluated in a proper perspective. These 'experiences' must be explained in a scientific manner to give a wider acceptance to Vastushastra. As the well-known mathematician and scientist Poincare had pointed out, "Science is built up of facts, as a house is built up of stones; but an accumulation of facts is no more a science than a heap of stones a house."

Even after granting the super science status to Vastushastra, efforts should be made to explain the logic and 'why' behind each of its tenets, edicts and principles. There is this famous rule by *William of Occam*, also known as *Occam's Razor*: *"Entia non sunt multiplacanda praeter necessitatem"*, loosely translated in English as "Neither more, nor more onerous causes are to be assumed than are necessary to account for the phenomenon."

Sir Isaac Newton in his book *Principia* echoes a similar type of logic through the statement : "No more causes of natural things are to be admitted than such as are both true and sufficient to explain the phenomenon of these things."

The causes behind the principles and edicts enunciated in Vastushastra must be researched in the light of the above basic rules governing cause and effect. Even after assuming that every edict, every principle of Vastushastra is a God-spelt truth, attempts must be made to present the reasoning behind these rules in a scientific manner.

One can come to a conclusion that a particular problem has no solution. But the position taken by some of the rationalists that the science of Vastushastra has no basis at all, that no attempt should be made to explain the mysterious working of cosmic forces at work, is entirely incorrect. In fact, every possible tool available in modern theoretical and experimental science should be used to understand the scope and application of Vastushastra for the benefit of the common man.

Knowledge about Vastushastra has generally been a jealously guarded secret. Any new work on Vastushastra discipline should go beyond mere compilation of rules and description of success stories, and should aim at an indepth theoretical and experimental analysis. Only an urge from within to understand the scientific logic behind the mysterious rules that more often than not provide practical solutions to problems encountered by human beings in their journey through life, can help in dissemination of the limited information available on Vastushastra.

In a broader sense, it can be said that Vastushastra encompasses not only cosmology and astronomy, but also astrology, physics, chemistry, and various yogic disciplines. In many Western countries studies are being carried out to explore fresh areas of human thought through research on cosmo-biological influence on human psyche. Vastushastra concepts deserve scientific analysis. We have to keep in mind that the entities termed as 'mysteries' in pre-atomic theory science have been explained in recent times through discoveries in modern physics. Vastushastra cannot lie hidden in a veil of mystery if modern scientific tools are applied for gaining deeper insights into this wonderful science.

3

YOGASHASTRA – MOTHER OF VASTU SCIENCE

Prana is the energy permeating the universe at all levels. It is physical, mental, intellectual, sexual, spiritual and cosmic energy. All vibrating energies are prana. All physical energies such as heat, light, gravity, magnetism and electricity are also prana. It is the hidden or potential energy in all beings, released to the fullest extent in times of danger. It is the prime mover of all activity. It is energy which creates, protects, and destroys. Vigour, power, vitality, life and spirit are all forms of prana.

—— B.K.S. Iyengar in 'Light on Pranayama'

Yogashastra has great relevence for Vastushastra. The concept of *prana* in Yogashastra permeates throughout the Vastushastra in the sense that Vastushastra considers every Vastu to be a living entity in the form of the *Vastu-Purush*. Once the basic concepts of Yogashastra are analysed and understood, we can examine the common philosophy governing these two ancient sciences.

Nabhi in Ayurveda, Yogashastra and Vastushastra

In the Ayurveda stabilising, fixing and aligning the *nabhi* (*nabhi*, i.e., navel, assumed to be the centre of the human body) is seen as the basic line of treatment with the firm belief that any medicine can have pronounced remedial action only if the *nabhi* is stable. In fact, a naturally centred *nabhi* is considered as a definite sign and indication of good health.

In Yogashastra, the *nabhi* is considered as the source of all good things, and the *Ganesh-beej*, the harbinger of all activities, is said to be located at that point. In the *Puranas*, the *nabhi* is seen as the abode of 'Brahma' and is assumed to be a source of all creation. The primary energy-life relation between a mother and a child is established through the umbilical chord (having a helix form) originating from the *nabhi* itself. In a different context, the subject of *nabhi* permeates throughout the Vastushastra. The conceptual relevance of *nabhi* for planning a Vastu, apart from the importance of helix shape in Vastushastra has been discussed in detail in the chapter on dynamic balance.

Ida-Pingala Nadis in Yogashastra and Vastushastra

A recurring theme in *Pranayama* as practised in Yogashastra relates to the subject of *nadis* (streams). Depending on the functional aspect, some of these *nadis* as visualised in Yogashastra may correspond to arteries, veins, capillaries of the respiratory and circulatory systems as defined in modern physiology and anatomy.

The most important *nadis* are considered to be *Ida, Pingala* and *Shushubhna*. Swami Vivekananda has explained this concept in simple words:

The sun current (*Pingala*) and the moon current (*Ida*) bring energy to all parts of the body. The surplus energy is stored at certain points, plexuses, along the spinal column, commonly known as nerve centres. A third, the *Shushubhna*, is a very fine, very brilliant thread, a living passage through the spinal cord, through which the *Kundalini* rises.

Similar concepts are found in Vastushastra. The North-East directional flow considered *Shubh* (auspicious) in Vastushastra is attributed to *Ida, the moon* current. The South-West is assumed to be *Ashubh* (inauspicious) direction on account of *Pingala, the sun* current.

Chakras, or "plexuses of consciousness" form the major nerve ganglia of an extraordinary circuitry of *nadis*, energy channels that link together our animal body with our subtler bodies and their higher functions like intelligence and love. It is because of these *chakras* and *Nadis* that our five *koshas* (intra-body sheaths or partitions) function smoothly and intelligently as one organism and 'awareness' can move through all bodies transiting from physical to emotional, to intuitional, to spiritual instantaneously.

Hindu (Vedic), Chinese (Taoist) and Tibetan (Buddhist) scriptures refer to an electrical human network of 72,000 *sukshma prana nadis* or subtle channels of vital force. The *Shiv Samhita* lists fourteen major currents. The important three — *ida, pingla,* and *shushubhna* running interwoven around and within the spinal cord — can be termed as super information highways. Yogis have visualised the *chakras* at the point of intense convergence of the *nadis*. The most important *chakras* are the seven above the base of the spine — *muladhara, svadisthana, manipura, anahata, visudha, ajna* and *sahasrara*. Some yogis experience and describe these *chakras* as whirlpools of light. These perform the basic function of receiving, filtering, polarising, focusing and distributing the vital life force *prana* throughout the body. It is now an accepted fact in bio-physics that in the human body, cell to cell communication and the DNA command signals utilise polarised ultraviolet light as medium of transmission.

Our five *koshas* — physical, vital *(pranic)*, emotional (mental), intuitive (cognitive) and super-consciousness are beautifully interlocked like layers of an onion *(kanda)*. Each one is encased by the next subtler layer as they function together in our daily consciousness. The body maintains a connection with each of the *chakras* through the nerve ganglia along the spinal cord and cranium. Physical nerves are generally measured in terms of micrometre or millimetres, but these subtle nerves *(sukshma nadis)* and *chakras* are visualised in terms of vibrations akin to short-wave radio frequencies. It has been experimentally verified by experts in the fields of bio-physics and medicine that intensity of a signal is transmitted through neurons in terms of increase or decrease of frequency, rather than amplitude variation. This fact was perhaps known to the seers codifying Yogashastra and Vastushastra, and was suitably adopted for maintaining a healthy body and mind, and for constructing houses in tune with the cosmic forces.

The fact to be noted is that Vastushastra with all its mystic secrets is a super-science that systematically attempts to provide guidelines for building houses that are environment-friendly, the dwellings which are free of destructive radiation and the structures with internal atmosphere in harmony with cosmic forces and conducive to friction-less flow of *prana* through *sukshma nadis* and *chakras*.

Prana in Body and Cosmic Energy in a Vastu

The flow of *prana* through a human body and the flow of cosmic energy through a Vastu are in essence parallel concepts.

According to the Yogashastra, the universe is composed of two substances: *akash* (ether) and *prana* (cosmic energy). Everything which has a form, or is the result of a combination evolves out of the *akash*. It is the *akash* that becomes the air, liquids, solids, the human body, animals, plants, etc. Everything we can touch, all the forms we see, everything that exists can be sourced to the *akash*. It is so subtle that we cannot perceive it, for it is only visible once it has taken form. The power by which it is transformed into the universe is *prana*.

Everything we call energy or force evolves out of *prana*. In all forms of life, from the highest to the lowest, the *prana* is present as a living force. Every force is based on *prana*, it is the origin of movement, gravity, magnetism, physical action, the nerve currents and the force of thought. *Prana* is the soul of all force and energy and there can be no life without it. It is found in the air, water and food. *Prana* is the vital force inside each living being, and 'thought' is considered to be the highest and the most refined action of *prana*. *Prana* is said to concentrate at the point where our mind is focussed.

प्राणो ब्रह्मेति व्यजानात् *(Prano Brahmeti Vyajanat)*. In *Taitariya Upanishad* it is said that the whole existence is based on *prana*, is part of *prana* and it ends in *prana*. *Prana* belongs to one of the five elements of *Panch Maha Bhutas*, i.e., *vayu*. It exists in the human body in five more types: *Prana, Apana, Vyan, Udan* and *Saman*. These five are correlated with five basic elements — *Akash, Vayu, Tej, Udak* and *Prithvi*.

Existence of cosmic energy in a human body is the amalgamation of these five elements with the five *pranas*. *The Home,* the Vastu which serves as a shield for the human body, is taken care of by Vastushastra on the same basic logic that applies to *panch-pranas* and the five basic elements. Basic rules and regulations in *Shiv Swarodaya Shastra* to preserve and enlighten the 'Godliness' in human body are applicable to Vastushastra also. The science of Yoga maintains a correlation between existence, reality and truth by the effective flow of *panch-prana*. The rules of Vastushastra beneficially applied, attempt to maintain balance with cosmic reality, to illuminate intelligence and to attain peace by following *perfect directions, perfect magnetic flux and perfect correlation of the basic five elements* (refer to fig. 3.1, 3.2, 3.3).

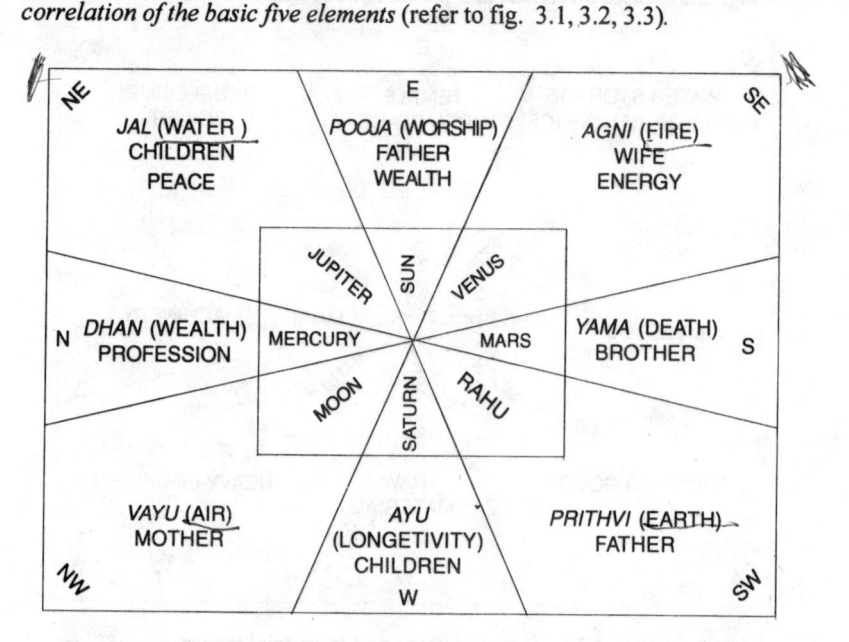

Fig. 3.1 : Vastu directions, *Panch-Maha-Bhutas* and governing planets.

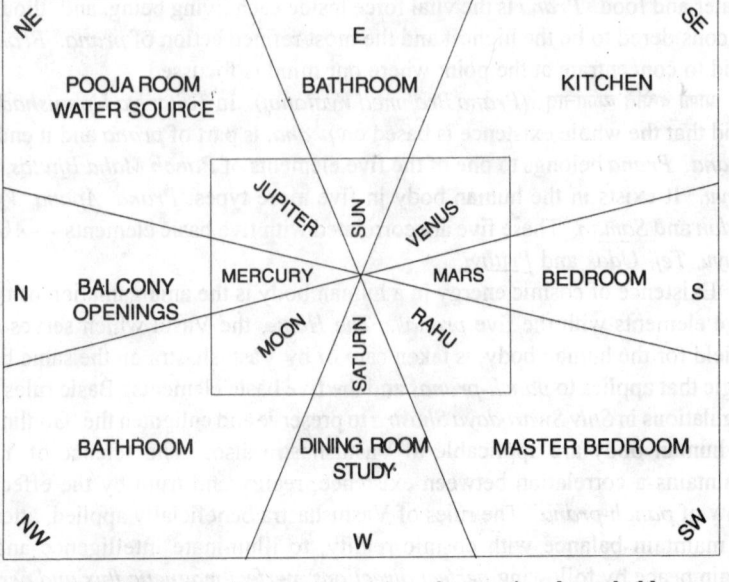

Fig. 3.2 : Vastu directions and planning of rooms in a household.

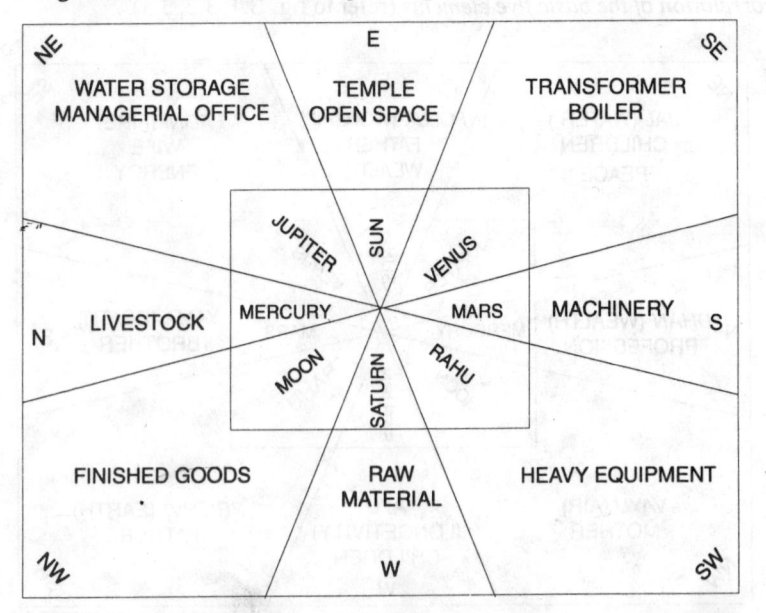

Fig. 3.3 : Vastu directions and industrial layout.

Nadi Excitation and Directions of a Vastu

According to an old treatise on Yogashastra, the human body is constituted by 72,000 energy channels, termed as *nadis*. Amongst these five types of *pranas* or *vayus* flow. According to the demands of the work to be performed, a logical play of a particular *vayu* takes place in a specific *nadi*. The three most important *nadis* are known as *Ida (Chandra Nadi), Pingala (Surya Nadi),* and *Shushubhna (Brahma Nadi).*

Ida current flows when we breathe through the left nostril. *Pingala* exits when we breathe through the right nostril. *Shushubhna* manifests itself at the time of change of duties of *Ida* and *Pingala.*

Ida has control over East and North directions (fig. 3.4). All good things, all creative works, arts and research, religious and life promoting activities are attributed to the flow of *Ida Nadi* (left or northern current flow). *Pingala,* i.e., *Surya Nadi* has control over West and South directions (fig. 3.4). All violent activities, all destructive forces, deployment of weapons, tortures, sorrows, cruel and tough jobs, worldly attractions are attributed to the flow of *Surya* or *Pingala Nadi* (right or South flow). *Brahma* or *Madhyam Nadi* represents only the holy and devotional duties, i.e., reading religious scriptures, meditation, prayers and absence of worldly material activities. In other words, maintaining *Ida* flow is good, divine and worldly bliss. To block *Pingala* flow is to avoid any destruction and disturbances. Similarly, Vastushastra recommends that maximum space should be left open towards the North and the East directions and that the Vastu should be aligned in the South and the West zones. Provision of more space in the North and the East directions ensures that the entire household is exposed to health-preserving energy of clear morning sun for the maximum possible duration. Maximum openings to the East and the North maintain and shower this bliss on the whole house. Absence of openings to the South and the South-West as stated in Vastushastra, cross-ventillates this positive energy from the East to the North, and like a circular flow, from the North to the East. For, a house with minimum side margins to the South and the West on the rearside, effectively blocks any *Pingala Nadi* current and adds all good effects of *Ida Nadi* by maintaining flow in the North and the East directions only. To achieve the dynamic stability by equalising gravitational forces, magnetic flux effect and to attain environmental purity and a sense of cosmic reality, the major load of the house should be aligned to the South and the West zones of the plot.

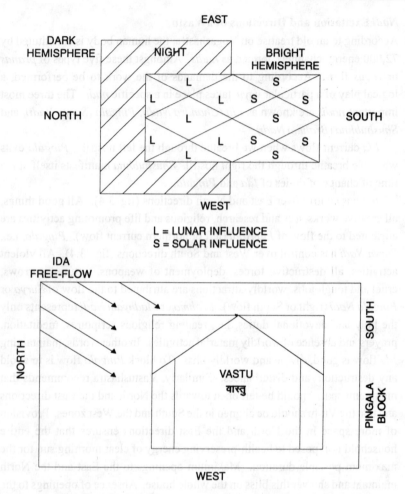

Fig. 3.4 : *Ida* **(Lunar current) control over North and East.**

As seen in previous chapters, a loaded South can absorb the cosmic elementary particles travelling along the magnetic field lines and can reduce the deleterious micro radiations. Thick walls without openings on the South side provide a shield to the household against this destructive cosmic force.

\ Yogashastra asserts that just by maintaining a perfect posture of body, substantial qualities are added to body, mind and intellect. Similarly, simple alignment and positioning of a house in the proper zone of a plot as per Vastushastra can add several qualities to the house or a dwelling.

Five Basic Elements in Yogashastra and Vastushastra

In Yogashastra, the flow of *prana* in the body is correlated with the virtues of five basic elements, and the qualities of five elements in relation to human body are also defined. Colour, shape, taste and smell of five elements are categorised in Yogashastra. Amongst these colours, shapes, tastes and smells Vastushastra defines qualities associated with *Prithvi* and *Jal tatva* as good and those with *Agni-Tej* as unhealthy, while qualities with *Vayu tatva* are considered as inert. This classification matches the scientifically analysed mineral content in the soil acceptable for use in the base of the Vastu.

Any abode demands contribution of all the qualitative parameters like colour, taste, shape, form, sound and touch. All these qualities are attributed to *Prithvi tatva* alone. Hence, Vastu science gives importance to influencing expression of *Prithvi tatva*. Here, we see how foundations of Vastu concepts have been derived from Yogashastra. A deep understanding and right selection makes it possible to match definitions in Yogashastra and applications in Vastushastra.

Drawing from the Yogashastra insight, Vastushastra allots specific characteristics to the five basic elements. The element 'Earth' is visualised as yellow-coloured, 'Water' as white, 'Fire' as red, 'Wind' as blue, and 'Ether' as having no definite colour property, to have to borrow colour from any other element.

The classification and characteristics of these elements can be described in terms of *varna* (colour), *akar* (shape), *swad* (taste) and *guna* (quality).

Table 3.1: Characteristics of Five Basic Elements

Element (Tatva)	Colour (Varna)	Shape (Akar)	Taste (Swad)	Quality (Guna)
Earth (*Prithvi*)	Yellow	Square / Rectangle	Sweet (*Madhur*)	Good
Water (*Jal*)	White	Semicircle	Salty (*Turat*)	Good
Fire (*Agni*)	Red	Triangle	Hot (*Tikshna*)	Inert
Air (*Vayu*)	Blue / Black	Circle	Acidic (*Amla*)	Bad
Ether (*Akash*)	Not defined	None	Bitter (*Kadu*)	Bad

Vastushastra begins with the selection of a plot and type of soil, qualifies shapes suitably conforming to the cosmic balance of *Prithvi tatva* — the Earth element. In categorising qualities of soil to suit cosmic balance, *Jal tatva* is considered good, *Agni tatva* as inert and *Vayu tatva* as unacceptable. As explained earlier, squares and rectangles exhibit the typical perfect balance as the magnetic flux is uniaxial (fig. 3.5).

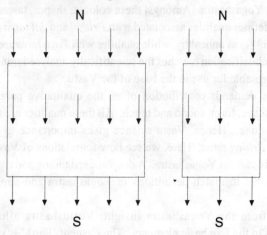

Fig. 3.5 : Square and rectangular plots are dynamically balanced.

The shape defined for the earth element is a square or a rectangle. All the other shapes being dynamically unbalanced are considered as useless. From the chart we can observe that only *Prithvi* element is considered good.

In Vastushastra the type of soil essential for selecting a plot and building a house should be white, yellow or at least red in colour. The taste recommended is sweet or at the most, slightly salty. White and yellow soils have natural pest-controlling qualities due to the presence of minerals like calcium, potassium, manganese, magnesium, etc. Water-logging possibility in these soils is characteristically low, offering natural plinth protection, avoiding differenial settlements and seasonal fluctuations. Due to white and yellow colours, the soil has good thermal insulating properties, reducing direct penetration of solar energy, resulting in benign environment around the house. Additionally, because of better bearing capacities for foundation of these soils, the construction proves to be economical.

On the other hand, black soils are a headache for the civil engineer and the occupants. A mineral called montmorillonite is abundant in black soils. The montmorillonite crystals have very high swelling characteristics which result in differential settlement in foundations and expanding cracks in plinths. Due to the black colour, the soil has poor thermal insulation and it holds and stores during daytime, the direct penetrated solar energy which emanates out in the shadow period of night, resulting in very unhealthy environment throughout the day. Due to high absorption of solar energy, magnetic flux lines in the zone are disrupted leading to complete cosmic disorder all around. Perceiving these characteristics in their entirety, soils with blue-black colour and of acidic taste, i.e., soils having *Vayu tatva* nature are totally proscribed by Vastushastra in selection of a plot.

As discussed previously, the Yogashastra concepts of *prana, nabhi, nadi, chakra, panch-maha-bhutas,* and *panch-koshas* have definite correlation with principles of Vastushastra. In Yogashastra, the *Shanmukhi Mudra* provides the body with qualities of *panch-maha-bhutas* (five basic elements) and three important streams or current *Ida, Pingala* and *Shushubhna* are associated with qualities of directions. Vastushastra essentials are based on contributions from the *panch-maha-bhutas* and *directions,* concepts basically associated with Yogashastra. Again in Astrology, *direction* is an important aspect with the directionally located *rashis* (zodiac) and *nakshatras* (constellations) having qualities of *panch-maha-bhutas.* Further, the recommended *aradhyavrikshas* (beneficial plants) for a given constellation have associated with them, definite colours, rhythms and qualities of the five basic elements. The chart given here indicates the observed correlation between Yogashastra, Astrology and Vastushastra.

Table 3.2 Vastushastra Correlation with Yogashastra, Astrology, Science

Yogashastra	Astrology	Vastushastra	Modern Science
Shanmukhi mudra gives knowledge about qualities of the five great basic elements. The three main energy streams categorise the virtuous qualities of the eight directions. *Ida* (Chandra *Nadi*) – North-East *Pingala* (Surya *Nadi*) – South-West *Sushubhna* (Brahma *Nadi*) – Central Zone	The cosmos is divided into basic eight directions with twelve sectors of the zodiac signs. These signs are classified on the basis of five basic elements. The directions are then correlated with qualities of the five great basic elements interpreted in terms of beneficial colours, plants, gems and metallic base elements.	Vibrations, waves, sound, and light are the active parameters in this science. Qualities are classified, based on orientation, directions and energy sources. Qualities of directions can be improved on the basis of the five great elements.	Explains qualities of • polarised energy forms, • laws of energy conservation, • mind-matter relationship. Modern science unveils the secrets of ancient science, and gives new remedial measures to rectify *Vastudoshas* and to provide environmental enrichment.

It will not be out of place to discuss here some of the intricate problems of mind-body correlation observed by modern day practitioners of medicine. On a subtle level these problems have relevence to and may find answers in Yogashastra and Vastushastra.

Sanskara in Vastushastra and Quantum Memory in Medicine

Dr Deepak Chopra in his book *Quantum Healing* discusses experiments carried out by French immunologist Dr Jacques Benveniste, wherein it was discovered that the human body's immune system can be triggered not only by actual presence of certain agents, but also through 'memory' of these agents retained by water molecules even after the solution had undergone the dilution process a number of times to remove any trace of the agent. The actual experiment consisted of mixing human blood serum full of white cells and IgE (immunoglobulin E type antibody) with a solution prepared from goat's blood (containing anti-IgE agent) to trigger the release of histamine. Even after diluting the anti-IgE to about 1 part antibody to trillion, trillion parts water, the pattern of reaction remained unchanged, i.e., the histamine release retained the same degree of intensity. The inference drawn was, "the human white cells were acting as if anti-IgE was attacking them from everywhere when in fact it was nowhere."

In vaccination, dead germs or dead bacteria in suitable dilutions are introduced into the human body so that the immune system can be trained to produce the necessary antibodies to fight these and the actual live strains having similar molecular structure. In this process also some sort of memory mechanism of the body is made operative.

Homoeopathy follows a symptoms-based line of treatment rather than directly dealing with actual organisms causing the disease. Using an elaborate system of poisons and toxic herbs that mimic the symptoms of a true disease, homoeopathic treatment gives the body a simulated taste of illness to be cured.

In the light of Dr Deepak Chopra's elaborate arguments we can infer that not only a living cell in the human body, but even a tiny molecule in a living organism has some sort of intelligence and memory susceptible to methodical training and conditioning.

Systematic conditioning of body and mind at cellular level is indeed achieved, if the dwelling in which a man spends his maximum living hours is designed as per the tenets of Vastushastra. The aim of Vastushastra is to create congenial conditions for the human body and mind so that the man can live in harmony with nature and the cosmic forces. Prosperity and wealth are secondary effects only, achieved by the body that can withstand abnormal conditions and by the mind that can take right decisions because it is in tune with the cosmos. In the next chapter, we will see how to correlate qualities of the five elements explained in Yogashastra with zodiac signs as defined and classified in Astrology.

4

INSIGHT OF ASTROLOGY AND
VASTUSHASTRA ANALYSIS

The First Morning of Creation wrote
What the Last Dawn of Reckoning will read.

Astronomy and Vastushastra

Before the discovery of magnetic compass, ancient cultures had always used heavenly bodies and astronomical observations for locating directions. From the heavenly bodies these cultures derived their cosmic view of life. The integrated man-spirit-cosmos view evident in ancient Chinese, Egyptian, and Mayan cultures has in fact been the backbone of Indian philosophy and outlook towards life in general. Man, the thinker, occupies a distinct place in the Indian perception of nature. The Vedic rishis put forward their cosmic view through the concepts like *purush* (cosmic element), and *prakriti* (nature). Shri B.K.S.Iyengar in his book *Light on Pranayama* has commented:

"Purusa is the universal psychic principle, which though unable to perform any action by itself, animates and vitalises nature (*prakriti* or the producer), the universal physical principle, which through its three qualities and evolutionary powers (*gunas*) produces intellect (*buddhi*) and mind (*manas*). *Purush* and *prakriti* acting together stir the material world to activity. Both are limitless, without beginning or end."

The Indian Vedic view considers the cosmic energetic source as a procreator of all the manifest world. There is also a concept of the Light-Infinite beautifully described in various forms by Sri Aurobindo in his book *Savitri*. In the *Upanishads* the *Brahman* is referred to as the 'Self-Luminous Light'. In this system, the sun, the moon, the planets and the stars are assumed as the manifest entities originating from the infinite light source.

Vastushastra goes deeper into these concepts to understand the true significance of the sun, the moon, the planets and the stars in terms of cosmic energy fields and cosmic forces at play and the resultant micro-effects on

nature and human life. The edicts of Vastushastra evolved ou\
humanitarian outlook that sought to ensure a harmonious life which
with nature and the cosmos for the entire mankind.

Correlation between Vastushastra and Astrological Analysis

Astrology predicts the future on the basis of deficiencies in any given horoscope
(see Table 4.4) and correlating these with faults of individual body and
consciousness. Astrological inferences are based on the relative and the
combined force-fields of planets acting on an individual consciousness.
Positions of planets in a particular direction have an effective and definite
control on human endeavour and future events. After all, it is the combination
of various gravitational and allied forces, that gives rise to a particular situation.

In the same way, a house built on a particular plot has direct correlation
with the electromagnetic forces and the gravitational fields of earth and other
planets together with forces /effects of cosmic origin. Understanding of these
forces and energy fields as counter-balanced by gravitational mass (load) to
attain dynamic balance, is the basic philosophy of Vastushastra. Since human
consciousness has a direct relationship with the house occupied by the
individual, this affinity of the house and the dweller is amplified to predict the
eventualities for the house and the person on the basis of logical fibre of
Astrology and Vastushastra (refer to Table 3.2).

Vastu Purush Mandal

In Vastu Purush Mandal, two sources of energies or cosmic forces are designated
by symbolic nomenclature which refers to the positive or negative confluence
of these forces leading to positive, conformable and lively results, or negative,
retrograde and destructive results as symbolised by the names of deities ruling
various directions in Vastu Purush Mandal. In ancient texts, the positive
confluence is termed as "प्रीति संगम" (Priti Sangam) indicating dynamic additive
flow of both the forces in the direction of propogation, while the negative
confluence is termed as "विष संचार" (Visha Sanchar) meaning thereby that the
forces are turbulent and flow in opposite directions to each other trying to
annihilate the other force. The two sources of force and energy field are :
(1) solar energy termed as "प्राणिक" (Pranic) energy or the cosmic energy, and
(2) electromagnetic flux termed as "जैविक" (Jaivic) energy or the organic energy.

Pranic or the solar force field can be represented as an everchanging dynamic
vector referenced to solar position and moves through 360 degrees in relation
to the earth's position. On the other hand, Jaivic or organic force field is

unidirectional with vectors directed from North to South poles. Friendship, reinforcement or union of these forces is ideal 'heavenly' condition. Oneness of *Pran* and *Jeev* is termed as life. Any inimical or contradictory association of these forces results in pain, hardship and sorrow. *Jeev* devoid of *Pran* is termed as death.

Vastu Purush Mandal and Modern Science

Darshanshastra (दर्शनशास्त्र) is the outcome of comprehensive perception of nature. Logical statements may fail to match the reality, but not perception. Comprehensive perception is the expression of reality manifested through oneness of observer, observed and observation. In man's quest for truth, Darshanshastra leaves the "cause-effect relationship" way behind in terms of the contents and the results. It is the expression of order of nature and not to the manipulation of a clever mind. The perception evolving after dismantling of cultural ethos based on stereotypes and categorisation, is also termed as bliss.

Darshanshastra explains and narrates the state of human existence as a stream of consciousness defined as सत् चित् आनंद (*Sat-Chit-Ananda*). The term *freedom* is inadequate here, as it projects an image of a shackled human being.

The five *Upangas* (sub-branches) of Darshanshastra are basically various applied engineering sciences which formulate the comprehensive perception in terms of cause-effect, matter-energy, and substance-body. The five *upangas* can be tabulated as follows;

Table 4.1 Disciplines Branching out of Darshanshastra

DARSHAN SHASTRA

|
Upangas (Sub-branches)

|

SANGEET	JYOTISHA	AYURVEDA	YOGASHASTRA	VASTUSHASTRA
Music	Astrology	Medicine		
|	|	|	|	|
Notes	*Yoga*	*Nadi*	*Pran*	*Prithvi*
Beats	*Muhurta*	*Sama-Ushna*	*Mudra*	Sun
Rhythm	Energy	*Sheet-Tap*	*Vayu*	*Vayu*

These elements create the necessary energy fields for existence, evolution and development of life. The sub-branches of Darshanshastra prepare the fertile ground for the seed of *Sat-Chit-Ananda* to flower and evolve into a lifelong experience.

The Vastu Purush Mandal can be interpreted in terms of two scientific concepts: (1) vector analysis of changing directional solar energy flux superimposed on North-South geomagnetic flux and the resultant energy fields, (2) interaction of elementary particle flux with North-South electromagnetic field lines.

The term *Jaivic Urja* (organic energy) in ancient scripts refers to the North-South geomagnetic flux. These field lines orient and fix energy centres in living organisms. This eternal unidirectional flow defines, propagates and directs the 'existence' at a cellular level in all living entities. The *Pranic Urja* (cosmic energy) refers to the highly energetic solar energy flux, the intensity of which varies with the relative position of the sun with respect to the earth (Fig. 4.1).

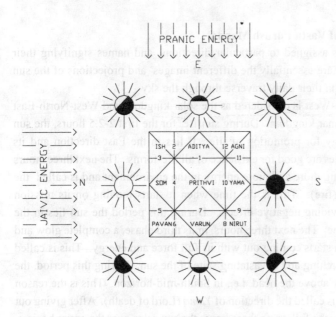

The dark portion of the solar disk indicates the relative intensity of solar flux received by the earth, i.e., from the South direction the earth receives the maximum amount of solar energy, etc.

Fig. 4.1: Vastu Purush Mandal in terms of *Jaivic* and *Pranic Urjas*.

e 'deities' governing various directions in Vastu-Purush-Mandal denote the positive or negative confluence of the *Jaivic Urja* and *Pranic Urja* fluxes brought about by changing position of the sun in its daily sojourn through the sky.

The South-East (*Agni*), South (*Yama*), and South-West (*Gagan*) are mythologically represented as "शिव–तांडव" (Shiv-Tandav) or the demonic dance. The North (*Som*), North-East (*Ish*) and East (*Aditya*) are represented as "चिद्–विलास" (*Chid-Vilas*), or the mind-play. As such, the North-East is termed as the source of all energies and the South-West is termed as the sink of all the energies. The vector connecting North-East to South-West is assumed to be the *Life-diagonal* or the *Energy-diagonal* defining the borderline between the zones of good effects and bad effects. It is a good Vastushastra practice to ensure that the *Bramhasthal* or the *Vastu-Nabhi* (discussed in detail elsewhere in the book) is located towards the South-West on the lower one-third of this life-diagonal.

Significance of Vastu Purush Mandal

The goddesses assigned to particular directions, and names signifying their characteristics are essentially the different images and projections of the sun and the moon in their daily traverse through the sky.

East-South-West is considered as the solar kingdom and West-North-East is called the lunar kingdom. During sunrise, for the first 2-2.5 hours, the sun provides energy for promotion of life. It lies in the East direction and its primary energies are good for existence of all life-forms. The next three hours it starts radiating more and more energy in the environment and is called the state of *Agni* (fire). This is the time when it starts moving on its mission gradually, providing negative effects. During this period the sun lies in the South-East zone. The next three hours, in its third phase, a complete glow and aura of the sun starts coming out with its full force and energy. This is called *Yama* — a scorching and devastating state of the sun. During this period, the sun lies exactly above the head, i.e., in South-mid-horizon. This is the reason why the South is called the direction of *Yama* (Lord of death). After giving out all its radiation, the following three hours the sun rules over the entire horizon with its complete command. This is called *Gagan,* a state associated with sorrow due to the sun's excess thermal activity and its location in the South-West. At sunset it cools down and directs its rays towards the moon for its night-reign.

Insight of Astrology and Vastushastra Analysis

In fact, the Vastu Purush Mandal represents images of goddess
to the effects of the sun and its position in that particular direction (
4.2B). With reference to the cosmic environment, these images exactly fit the
sun's position in the sky.

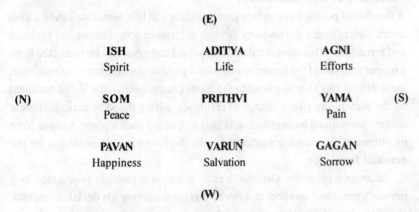

(E)

ISH	ADITYA	AGNI
Spirit	Life	Efforts

(N)

SOM	PRITHVI	YAMA	**(S)**
Peace		Pain	

PAVAN	VARUN	GAGAN
Happiness	Salvation	Sorrow

(W)

Fig. 4.2.A : Deities governing eight directions in Vastu Purush Mandal.

VASTU PURUSH MANDAL

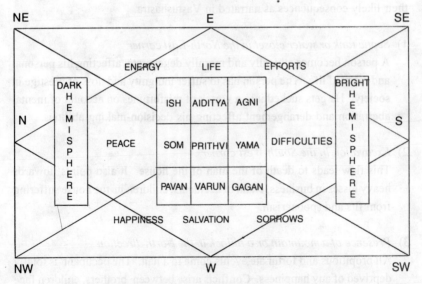

Fig. 4.2B : Vastu Purush Mandal significance of deities.

A similar but positive pattern of cosmic reality is seen in the half circle of the moon travel and accordingly, images of goddesses are assigned to the particular direction in Vastu Purush Mandal.

Vastudoshas and Calamities

A number of people have to face great hardships in life, sometimes even a total destruction of house and property through unforeseen acts of nature like cyclones and tornadoes. This typical calamitous period can generally be predicted from a proper analysis of the horoscope of such a person. As a matter of coincidence, these effects can also be traced to the flaws (vastudoshas) in a Vastu occupied by the person, say after a change of residence, during the same period. If these defects are noticed beforehand, it is best to discard such a place, so as to limit or eliminate the damage associated with the future events predicted by the personal horoscope.

In an exceptionally virtuous Vastu, systematic changes take place in a person's mind and intellect at a micro level, reinforcing his decision- making abilities. Armed with decisive confidence, he can face any difficulty, calamity or catastrophy with a degree of courage and fortitude to emerge a winner.

We are enlisting here a few ominous vastudoshas (deficiencies/flaws) and their likely consequences as narrated in Vastushastra.

1) *Septic tank or water closet in the North-East corner*

    A person becomes ethically and morally degenerate, affecting his personal and married life. The person has to suffer indignity and loss of prestige in society. He gets sucked into a vortex of misfortunes on account of mental aberration and derangement affecting his decision-making abilities.

2) *Excavation in the South-West corner*

    This flaw leads to death of the man of the house. It also points towards heavy losses in business, chain of accidents, children in the house suffering from fits and spoonerism.

3) *Presence of a mountain or a hillock in the North direction*

    All propitious and fortunate events come to a halt. The occupant is totally deprived of any happiness. Conflicts arise between brothers, children face difficulties in their studies, persons suffer from strifes and mental tensions.

4. *Mismatch of magnetic axis and the geometric axis*
   This flaw results in confusion creeping into all activities and hindrances in all planning. Disturbed health of the owner is noticed without any particular reason.

5. *A well in the South-East corner*
   Health hazards, problems in progeny and losses due to friends is attributed to such type of deficiency.

6. *Descending slope towards the South direction*
   Continuous erosion of wealth and financial losses, business and partnership problems and disturbed health of father of the owner can result from this *dosha.*

7. *Vyaghramukh (tiger-faced trapezoid plot) in the South.*

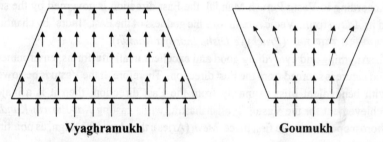

Vyaghramukh   **Goumukh**

Fig. 4.3 : *Vyaghramukh* **(tiger-faced) plot results in stress concentration.**
Goumukh **(cow-faced) plot allows for stress relief**

Sudden demise of close relatives through accidents, change of business with attendant unrest and health problems are foretold due to this type of flaw.

Directions, Flaws in Vastu and Remedial Measures
We have so far analysed rules of the Vastushastra as reflected in Science, Yogshastra and Jyotishshastra. On each and every Vastudosha (defect or a flaw in the Vastu), it is possible to find a remedial measure, provided that we seriously examine the doctrines in these disciplines on a micro level. It is quite likely that simple solutions can be found through application of modern science understood in a proper perspective.

An exotic and qualitatively excellent Vastu can be designed if we grasp the effect of phases of the sun and the moon on a Vastu and apply Vastu Purush Mandal to do justice to the directional aspect as identified by it. Light is the visible part of the electromagnetic spectrum. By following the basic principles of electromagnetism, even the part not responsive to human senses can beneficially be used in a Vastu to ward off micro-effects related to cosmic radiation waves and particles. The rise and fall of ground levels, slopes resisting free flow of magnetic flux, the effect of *Agni* (fire) and *Yama* (death) positions of the sun on a Vastu, the drawbacks of *Ishanyacut* (truncated North-East) affecting the divine influence of the moon, *Vidhishul* (event impediment) with reference to a well or a water body, *Vyaghramukh* (tiger-faced trapezoid); all such flaws or defects can be rectified through the trilogy of *Yogashastra-Jyotishshastra-Science* to transform a deficient Vastu into a qualitatively superior structure and virtuous abode for the dweller.

East Direction

According to Vastu Purush Mandal, the East direction is governed by the sun in its *Aditya* form. Vedic rites invoke the goddess of the East, 'Indra' by chanting "प्राच्यै दिशे इंद्राय नमः" (*Prachyye Dishe Indraya Namah*).

Anything and everything good and excellent in all life-forms, environment and nature is sourced from the East direction. Therefore, if the Vastu is bestowed with benevolent bliss primarily from the East direction, then it is a major achievement for the Vastu. Jyotishshastra, while casting *Kal-Purush-Kundli*, (horoscope), treats the first place *Mesh* (Aries), the *Agni* (fire) sign, as pointing towards the East.

The first place is supposed to influence the matters relating to personality, intellect, composure and activeness. Therefore, the East direction is very important for the smooth functioning of the household.

The following deficiencies are likely to be noticed in the East direction:

1. *Ascending Slope towards the East, i.e., descending towards the West*

This type of slope proves to be an obstacle in the entire Vastu receiving the benefit of the sun's vital energy in the morning. It is to be noted that the vibrant, life-sustaining electromagnetic vibrations from the sun available only in first 2.5 hours immediately after sunrise, are likely to be interrupted by this reverse slope. Ancient scriptures associate the sun with sight सूर्यो मे चक्षुशी श्रित:

(Suryo Mey Chakshushi Shritah). Extending this logic, we can figuratively say that the Vastu goes blind in the absence of benevolent sunlight. Apart from this, the Vastu comes under a shadow instead of sunshine, a factor considered unhealthy and unhygienic in Vastushastra. To guard against such a situation, a relative rise or ascend towards the West should be provided in the landscaping at the planning stage. Tall trees are not advisable on the East side, while a row of eucalyptus trees can be planted on the West border. Any compound on the East border must either be made up of wire-mesh or it should be light in weight. Maximum of window openings or ventilators should be provided on the East side of the house, and the roof, if provided, should be inclining towards the East.

2. Blocked East direction

In ownership flats, four flats in four directions and a central staircase is the general layout. This can result in blockage of the East direction for one of the flats. This defect is to be viewed in terms effects of the flaw indicated under (1). The situation can be remedied through modified window layout and certain other changes as indicated in the accompanying schematic.

3. Sinking of a well in the East direction

Comparing the rise and the fall of the ground level in various directions, sinking of a well in the East direction is treated in Vastushastra as a loss of gravitational mass for the East. This aspect is reasonably tolerated in the overall picture. But some scriptures interpret it as a defect *(dosha)* forewarning infertility or problems for progeny. According to *Kal-Purush-Kundli* the *Agni* (fire) element gets polluted due to the water element of the well and this has direct bearing on *Simha* (Leo) sign which is governed by *Ravi* (Sun) and *Agni* element, which may lead to loss of progeny. It is advisable to cap such a well.

4. Purva-Vyaghra Vastukshetra (Tiger-faced plot with East-side cut)

This flaw can be taken care of by providing a rising slope towards the West in landscaping and construction of a solid stone wall or barricade on the West side to prevent loss of energy towards the West direction. For qualitative improvement in the 'West' factor, trees should be planted on the West side as per the demands of the *Tula rashi* (Libra) and the scheme suggested in *Avakahada Chakra*. The Vastu should be constructed on a plateau sloping towards the East and the loading on the East side should be reduced to the least extent possible.

The scheme suggested for dynamic reduction of loading can give excellent results in such a case. The consequences of flaws like 'excessive East' and 'excessive *Agni tatva*' (fire element) can greatly be diminished by providing a well in the East for an East-*Vyaghra* plot. The contra-effects of East can be counter-balanced by planting of trees on the East side, which are basically associated with the West direction in the Vastushastra.

South-East Direction

According to Vastu Purush Mandal, the sun appears in the morning sky, between 9.00 and 11.30 a.m., in the South-East direction in its *Agni* (fire) form. Vedic scriptures invoke *Agni* by chanting "अग्नेयै दिशे अग्नये नमः" (*Agneyye Dishe Agnaye Namah*). In nature, all the energy sources originate from Agni (fire element). As mentioned in the ancient texts, the motive force for all the five basic elements (*panch-maha-bhutas*) is provided by the *Agni* element.

Agni in a sense is a medium of signalling and communucation and as described in Vedic scriptures, "अग्निर्मे वाचि श्रितः वाग हृदये " (*Agnirmey Vachi Shritah Vag Hridaye*). As such any deficiency in the South-East direction implies either dumbness or incoherent talk. Referring to *Kal-Purush-Kundli*, the profit aspect of eleventh place and loss aspect of the twelfth place are both governed by the South-East direction. The *Agni* sits on a fence between the two. You can either offer the hand of friendship to it, or accept it as an adversary. In Jyotishshastra, South-East direction is very important, and any flaw attributed to it can result in harming of interests through friends, monetary loss, theft, robbery, debt, worries, scepticism, and disgrace in general.

1. Well in the South-East Direction

This flaw is interpreted as an obstruction to the fire element (*Agni tatva*) and is associated with the annihilation of offsprings which is foretold on the basis of horoscope casting practices, in which fifth house (progeny, etc.) is placed seventh from eleventh house governed by the South-East direction. A well in the South-East direction is treated as a primary defect since rise towards South-East is mandatory in Vastushastra. Negative effects of a Vastu get accentuated through this flaw. No relief is available, not even after planting of trees selected for the South-East direction by the *Avakahada Chakra*. A minor amelioration is possible by acquiring additional land on South-East side to mimic an effect of excess South-East and relative loading of South-East direction. The best solution is to cap the well.

2. Excess South-East Corner

This flaw can be remedied through the construction of a water fountain in the South-East side corner to counter the exessive fire element. The other solution is to plant trees, having divine affinity for the North-West direction or the water element in the South-East. It is possible to subtract the excessive South-East by providing a square fencing to the courtyard.

3. Truncated South-East

This type of deficiency has to be countered very carefully. All the remedies required for increasing the fire element have to be employed to get the requisite relief. A few examples are:

a) planting of trees having divine affinity for the South-East direction, in that direction.

b) painting the internal walls of the Vastu on the South-East side with colour shades indicated in the *Shri Ranga Chakra.*

c) loading the available space between the East and the South directions.

d) providing a fireplace in the tiny space between the East and the South sides, as per the dictates of *Uccha Ushna Jyoti Chakra.*

4. South-East Vidhishula

The remedy for this flaw is to provide the main entrance on the North-East side, as per the recommendations of *Dwar Nivesh Phal.* The intense energy stress on account of Vidhishula can be reduced by raising the South-East corner height. Provision of a pond or a water fountain or an open water surface in the North-East proves helpful. By reinforcing the good qualities of the other directions, the effects of South-East deficiency should be relatively reduced without attempting any direct changes in the South-East direction.

South Direction

The sun in this direction takes the form of *Yama* (Lord of Death) as per the Vastu Purush Mandal. The sun from its position in the Southern skies, during the mid-noon 1100-1430 hrs emits intense energy with the scorching heat spreading throughout the atmosphere. Vedic scriptures invoke this direction through the *mantra* " दक्षिणयै दिशे यमाय नमः" (*Dakshinayye Dishe Yamay Namah*).

The interruption of electromagnetic flux lines, combination of cosmic rays and radiation particles, uneven magnetic field due to thermal imbalance and fierce hot sun results in amalgamation of all the destructive forces and energies which are undesirable from Vastushastra point of view.

Jyotishshastra treats South as the abode of *Shani* (Saturn) and has assigned the sign *Makara* (Capricorn) to that direction. *Kal-Purush-Kundli* ascribes tenth house to the South direction. As such, the following events are foretold — loss of employment, closure of business, unstability, social disgrace, political failure, insomnia, father becoming a drunkard, loss of paternal protection, etc. The net result is directly influenced by the nature of deficiencies in the Vastu.

1. *Ground level sloping towards the South*
A rise towards the South generally implies added gravitational mass acting as a catalyst to regulate excessive uncontrolled energy. As against this, a slope towards the South creates imbalance in energy-mass equivalence. This flaw can be rectified by loading the South side of the plot in the landscaping itself. The compound wall on the South border should be thick and high. Apart from this, to control the atmospheric temperatures, trees which exhale water vapour, such as *audumber* and *neem*, should be planted on the South border of the plot.

2. *South Vyaghra*
This is a major flaw as per the Vastushastra. By referring to the sketch (Fig. 4.3), we can observe that the flux lines originating from the North direction get concentrated on a smaller surface in the South direction. This stress accentuation, deadly energy fluctuations induced by hot atmospheric conditions in the South, and cosmic rays acting in consonance with radioative particles give a death-like (*Yamasthan*) characteristic to South *Vyaghra* plots. To escape this type of situation, all the proven principles of Vastushastra have to employed:
a) The South should effectively be loaded through gravitational mass at the landscaping stage.
b) *Audumber* and *neem* family trees should be planted in the South direction.
c) Wherever possible, the plot should be trimmed suitably.
d) The South side wall of the Vastu should have a two-feet-thick stone construction with no openings for windows, doors, ventilators or otherwise.
e) A floor should be added on the South side.
f) A cavity wall should be provided on the South side.
   After implementing these remedial actions, the character of the Vastu should be closely monitored for a few days. If necessary, characteristic virtues of other directions should also be enhanced.

3. *Well on the South side*
This type of flaw creates a void in the South direction with the attendant reduction in loading and uneven weight and resulting in energy retardation and structural imbalance. But, the best solution is to cap the well and remove the defect.

4. *Entrance on the South side*
The effect of this flaw is minimised if the entrance is planned as per the *Dwar Nivesh Phal* (fig. 4.4) to compensate the deficiency in the gravitational mass. The plot, in general, should be trimmed and the direction of the door should be altered suitably.

South-West Direction

The effects of southern magnetic tail are pronounced in the South-West direction, requiring heavy compensation through gravitational loading. All the remedial measures necessary for improving the characteristics of the South direction are mandatory in this direction. Only in case of a truncated South-West side, the space between the South and the West directions should be loaded heavily.

'द्वारनिवेश फल'

पू

	दु: खम्	शोकः	धनम्	नृपमान्यम्	महद दभयम	स्त्रि जन्म	अपुत्रता	हानि:	
शोक प्राप्ति:									मरणम्
दु:खम्									बन्धनम्
प्राप्ति:									भीति:
सुखागम:									पुत्रा प्ति:
संपत्ती:									धना-गम्
हानि:									यशो-लब्धि
महद दु: खम्									चौरा भयम्
श वृद्धि									व्याधि भीति
	शोकः	दु:खम्	धन लाभ	सौभाग्यम्	धना गम्	लक्ष्मी प्राप्ति:	स्त्रि-दु:खम्	निः स्वम्	

प

Fig. 4.4 : Classical *Dwar Nivesh Phal*

As per the *Kal-Purush-Kundli*, trees considered divine for countering *Vruschik* (Scorpion)-*Dhanu* (Sagittarius) type flaws, should be planted in the small area available between the South and the West directions. With heavy load on South-West side, the corresponding North-East direction should have open spaces. Inside the *Vastu* (structure), the painting scheme should adhere to *Shri Ranga Chakra*, especially in the cases involving cut in the South-West side.

In the *Kal-Purush-Kundli*, the South-West *doshas* (flaws) throw their shadow on the eighth house (associated with death) and the ninth house (prosperity), and as such, the flaws in this direction should be treated with due indulgence.

The Vastu Purush Mandal associates the South-West direction with the sun's *Gagan* form which is assumed to be microscopic sky element. Therefore, the contra-effects of flaws in the South-West direction are slow in acting, far reaching and not amenable to normal remedial measures. It is important that the defects in this direction are attended to, without any lethargy or prevarication.

West Direction

The Vastu Purush Mandal assigns *Varuna*, the rain-God, as the commander of the West direction. As per the Jyotishshastra, the radiationless hemisphere has its beginning in the West direction. Reign of the sun ends here, with the moon making an auspicious and propitious beginning. Jyotishshastra considers the minority group of the Moon, Venus and Jupiter as auspicious planets, while the Sun is assumed to be the source of evil influence. In the Vastu Purush Mandal, increasingly propitious and benevolent planet-goddesses appear sequentially, on the horizon, in the radiationless hemisphere governed by the Moon. In Jyotishshastra, this zone is dominated by benevolent third, fourth, and fifth houses which are propitious for knowledge and heavenly bliss.

Yogashastra infers that the current-flow *Ida* or *Chandranadi* which is indicative of auspicious elements and life-sustaining activities, governs the entire North direction.

Flaws in the West direction, associated with the seventh house in *Kal-Purush-Kundli*, are assumed to have bearing on marital bliss, separation from spouse, maternal protection, partnerships, legal matters, business, etc.

1. West Vyaghra

In this type of flaw, energy-flow towards the East direction is obstructed, as the West side is relatively larger than the East side. Since the energy is trapped on the East side, loading of the East as a counter-measure is totally ruled out because it may induce a fresh flaw in the nature of rise in level towards the East.

One of the solutions is to trim the plot and truncate the *Vyaghra* or the larger side. Or, the effect of loading on the East side can be simulated by placing the West and the East sides on an even level and removing any rise towards the West. Additionally, the benevolent characteristics of the other directions can be enhanced to bestow some good features on the Vastu.

2. Downward slope towards the West

This flaw can be tackled by providing a semblance of a slope towards the East at the landscaping stage. Loading of the West directions aids the free flow of electromagnetic energy.

3. Excess space towards the West

If excess open space is available on the West side, a maximum number of eucalyptus trees should be planted in that direction, with the remaining area to be covered by medicinal, herbal and aromatic plants and bushes.

Other Directions

The above procedure can also be followed for the North-West, North, and North-East directions for relief from the following types of Vastu defects:

   a) Cut in the North-West side.
   b) Excess North-West side.
   c) A well in the North-West direction.
   d) Rising slope towards the North-West.
   e) Rise towards the North.
   f) Obstruction in the North direction.
   g) North *Vyaghra* (tiger-faced trapezoidal plot).
   h) Cut in the North-East direction.
   i) Rise towards the North-East direction.

Additional relief measures include planting of trees having divine association with the direction, in that direction, as per the *Avakahada Chakra*, and using a scheme of painting for different directions of the Vastu indicated in the *Shri Ranga Chakra*.

According to *Kal-Purush-Kundli*, the wealth-related third, fourth, fifth and sixth houses are associated with the North-East, North, and North-West directions and their effects will be reflected through the flaws in the Vastu.

Important *Vastuchakras*

In cases where alterations in a Vastu are difficult to execute, remedies on *Vastudoshas* can be found in the various *Chakras* (schematics, charts, or tables) recommended by the Vastushastra. The *chakras* commonly used as reference are *Avakahada Chakra, Shri Ranga Chakra, Parinit Chakra,* and *Dwar Nivesh Phal,* along with the all encompassing Vastu Purush Mandal.

Shri Ranga Chakra and Colour Scheme for Painting

Every person has his preferences regarding various colours of nature. Colours can be pleasant or irritating depending on the personality involved. But, the underlying principle of *Shri Ranga Chakra* is the correlational pattern that can be defined between a colour shade and the virtuous qualities of the *panch-maha-bhutas, agni* (fire), *prithvi* (earth), *vayu* (air), *jal* (water), and *akash* (ether). In Jyotishshastra, the twelve astrological signs are assumed to have close affinity to a particular *tatva* (principle) of the five basic elements. The friendly or hostile relationship between various signs of zodiac and principal colours is indicated in Table 4.2.

Table 4.2 : The Zodiac Sign - Colour Schematic

Zodiac	Element	Colour	Soul-mate	Friend	Adversary
Aries Leo Sagittarius	Fire	Red	Air	Earth	Water
Taurus Virgo Capricorn	Earth	Yellow	Water	Fire	Air
Gemini Libra Aquarius	Air	Blue	Fire	Water	Earth
Cancer Scorpio Pisces	Water	White	Earth	Air	Fire

The colour schematic suggested here is useful in alleviating difficulties on account of *vastudoshas* in various directions. The methodology adopted for this purpose can be summarised as folows:

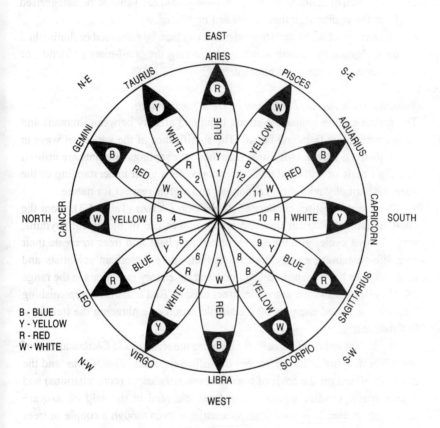

Fig. 4.5: *Shri Ranga Chakra*

a) Examine the Vastu thoroughly and determine the *vastudoshas* directionwise.
b) The 'polluted' zodiac sign should be verified from the directional aspect, with *Kal-Purush-Kundli* as the base.
c) The deficient element (of the *panch-maha-bhutas*) should be categorised from the zodiac sign that is polluted or diluted.
d) The net effect of the particular element can then be enhanced or diminished by designing the colour scheme considering the 'soul-mate', 'friend', or 'adversary' of the given element.

Avakahada Chakra and Selection of Trees for Planting
The Indian culture values the strong bond and affinity between humans and nature with all its flora and fauna. The significance of the variety of ways in which flowers, leaves, twigs, tree branches, tree saplings or plants are utilised in daily rituals or on religious occasions reveals a great understanding of the need for harmony with the environment and a great respect for nature.

There is a beautiful concept of *Avakahada Chakra* (Table 4.3), from the great Indian astrological tradition which makes use of biological rhythms, nature's own cycles and the ability of certain plants and trees to create their own life-sustaining energy fields. In fact, some American scientists and psychologists have been successful in detecting energy pulsations in the range 18-22 cycles per minute in the pine trees used by Red Indians for replenishing their own depleted energies by the simple action of embracing the tree for a few minutes.

The Indian ephemeris generally includes the *Avakahada Chakra* as one of the subjects. This *chakra* describes the influential *Nadi, Yoni, Gana* and the *Aradhyavriksha* on the basis of twenty-seven *nakshatras* (constellations) and twelve *rashis* (zodiac signs). The trees included in the said *chakra* are commonly available in the Indian subcontinent even though a couple of trees are specific to a particular region, soil-type and environmental growth factors. Even the *bonsai* form of the tree is quite effective for enhancing qualities of a given direction as per the Vastushastra considerations.

Out of the twenty-seven *nakshatras* (constellations), nine are from the *devagana* (divine type) : *Ashwini, Mriga, Punarvasu, Pushya, Hastha, Swati, Anuradha, Shravan* and *Revati*. The associated trees *Kuchli, Khair, Velu, Pimpal, Jayi, Arjun, Nagkeshar, Juyi* and *Moha* are recommended for plantings around the Vastu. Trees from the same botanical family can also be planted. One of the trusted methods is to place the earth at the centre of the *Kal-Purush-Kundli*

Table 4.3: *Avakahada Chakra*
(Zodiac - Constellation - Governing Tree - Basic Element)

Rahi Nakshatra (Zodiac Sign)	Aradhya Vriksha Element (Constellation)	(Benevolent Tree)	
Mesha (Aries)	Ashwini (Beta Arietis)	Kuchli	Air
	Bharani (Forty-one Aries)	Awali (*Emblica offi.*)	Fire
	Kritika 1 (Eta Tauri)	Umber	Fire
Vrishabha (Taurus)	Kritika 2,3,4 (Eta Tauri)	Umber	Fire
	Rohini (Alpha Tauri)	Jambhli (*Syzygium cu.*)	Earth
	Mriga 1,2 (Lambda Orionis)	Khair (*Prosopis ciner.*)	Air
Mithun (Gemini)	Mriga 3 4 (Lambda Orionis)	Khair (*Prosopis ciner.*)	Air
	Ardra (Alpha Orionis)	Krishngaru (*Acquilaria*)	Water
	Punarvasu 1 2 3 (Beta Geminorum)	Velu (*Dendro. Stricts*)	Air
Karka (Cancer)	Punarvasu 4(Beta Geminorum)	Velu (*Dendro. Stricts*)	Air
	Pushya (Sigma Cancri)	Pimpal (*Ficus religiosa*)	Fire
	Ashlesha (Alpha Cancri)	Nagchafa (*Mesua ferrea*)	Water
Simha (Leo)	Magha (Alpha Leonis)	Vat (*Ficus Bengalensis*)	Fire
	Purva (Delta Leonis)	Palas (*Butea monosper.*)	Fire
	Uttara 1 2 (Beta Leonis)	Dhayari (*Buxus sempe.*)	Air
Kanya (Virgo)	Uttara 2 3 4 (Beta Leonis)	Dhayari (*Buxus sempe.*)	Air
	Hastha (Delta Corvi)	Jayi (*Jasmin auriculata*)	Air
	Chitra 1 2 (Alpha Virginis)	Bel (*Aegle marmelos*)	Air
Tula (Libra)	Chitra 3 4 (Alpha Virginis)	Bel (*Aegle marmelos*)	Air
	Swati (Alpha Bootis)	Arjun (*Termindia arj.*)	Fire
	Vishakha 1 2 3 (Alpha Librae)	Nagkeshar (*Mesua fera*)	Earth
Vrischikh (Scorpio)	Vishakha 4 (Alpha Librae)	Nagkeshar (*Mesua fera*)	Earth
	Anuradha (Delta Scorpii)	Nagkeshar (*Mesua fera*)	Earth
	Jyeshtha (Alpha Scorpii)	Samber	Earth
Dhanu (Sagittarius)	Moola (Lambda Scorpii)	Ral (*Shorea robusta*)	Water
	Purvashadha (Delta Sagitarii)	Vet	Water
	Uttarashadha1(Alpha Sagitarii)	Phanas (*Jackfruit Tree*)	Earth
Makara (Capricorn)	Uttarashadha 2 3 4 (Alpha Sagitarii)	Phanas (*Jackfruit Tree*)	Earth
	Shravan (Alpha Acquilae)	Rui (*Gossypium arbo.*)	Earth
	Dhanishtha 12 (Beta Delphini)	Shami	Earth
Kumbha (Aquarius)	Dhanishtha 34 (Beta Delphini)	Shami	Earth
	Shatataraka (Lambda Acuarii)	Shami	Water
	Purvabhadrapada 1 2 3 (Alpha Pegasi)	Kalamb	Fire
Meena (Pisces)	Purvabhadrapada 4 (Alpha Pegasi)	Amra (*Mangifera ind.*)	Fire
	Uttarabhadrapada (Gamma Pegasi)	Kadulimb (*Azadiracta*)	Water
	Revati (Zeta Piscium)	Moha (*Madhuca lati.*)	Water

(horoscope) and arrange the *nakshatras* around it and then select the beneficial trees as per the zonal directions governed by the *nakshatras*. A slightly deeper analysis is required if trees are selected in the same manner as influential *ratnas* (gemstones) from the horoscope of the owner of the Vastu. It is possible to define the *dishadosh* (directional deficiencies) from the various aspects of the horoscope (see Table 4.4) and then determine the deficient element (out of the five basic elements) to select the relevant trees after considering the 'friend-adversary' effect of the affected element. For readers conversant with modern

Table 4.4 Effects of Various Houses in a Horoscope

House No.	Parameters influenced by the specific house in horoscope
1.	personality, nature likes/ dislikes, head, face, height, skin, colour, hair, rajyog
2.	facial expressions, family, expenses, ancestral property, shares, knowledge
3.	relatives, brotherhood, travel, voice, music, literature, reading, writing, bravery, mental illness, will power
4.	spouse, close friends, pet animals, material benefits, vehicle, vastu, agriculture, business know-how, aesthetics, flowers and fragrance, water-related items, chest, higher education, degrees, Godliness
5.	education, degree, learning, culture, love, marriage, devotion, dreams, artist, art, entertainment, theatre, racing, gambling
6.	enemies, problems in life, sorrow, company, job, civil servant, stomach, digestive system
7.	spouse, partnership, sexual life, kidney, lasciviousness, married life, divorce, competitors, entertainment, art, court matters, war
8.	death, difficulties, accidents, ancestral rights, dowry, corruption, illegal gains, Godliness
9.	religion, higher education, temple, philosophy, progress, guru/ guide, judge, court matters, vision, travel
10.	prestige, fame, promotion, rights, paternal backing business, job, knee, head, sleeplessness, social and political life, rajyog
11.	gains, jewellery, fashion, clothes, circle of friends, returns, left ear
12.	loss of property, financial crisis, penalty, punishment, feet, *moksha* sanyas, Godliness

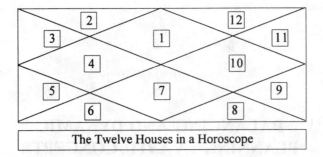

The Twelve Houses in a Horoscope

Western astronomy, we have indicated in the table above, the *nakshatras* and their Western astronomy equivalents.

The gemstones, the trees and colour combinations to complement the Vastushastra remedial actions can be selected with reference to these *nakshatras*. Sometimes it is advisable to seek some expert advice on these matters rather than relying on some informal unassimilated knowledge about the subject. Astrology and Vastushastra are complementary disciplines serving a wider purpose of harmonious life for all.

5

BALANCING AND DYNAMIC
PLANNING : VASTU CONCEPTS

The Cosmic Law is greater than thy will,
Even God Himself obeys the Laws he made,
The Law abides and never can it change,
The Person's a bubble on Time's sea

—*Sri Aurobindo in 'Savitri'*

The magnetic axis and the geometric axis of a Vastu play an important role in attaining good qualities and virtues in a Vastu. Unless these axes are parallel and colinear, the body movements inside the Vastu result in friction and high impedence to micro-magnetic fields of human body cells on account of oblique crossing of magnetic force lines through the medium. In all such cases where geometric axis of a plot is not parallel and colinear with geomagnetic axis, the architect should align the geometric axis of the house with the magnetic axis, giving a dynamic balance to the house.

The Importance of Shape in Vastushastra.
Every process in nature has a definite cause and purpose , every shape in nature has a definite effect and every existence in nature has a definite role to play. Environmental circumstances and conditions dictate the shape, size and other qualities of different living and non-living entities. Time and again, the naturally evolving shapes and sizes have proved their effectiveness even under continuously changing environmental factors.

Most of the man-made machines and systems are based on the observed similarities and the interpreted logical pattern in the naturally occurring substances. If we observe critically, we find that nature is a vast continuum. Its laws, regulations, causes and effects are interdependent and correlated to each other. In designing any new system or creating a new order, one has to search for its reflections in naturally existing substances which have proved their existence tenaciously by dynamically balancing the various forces in action.

If the cause and effect and the purpose are available in one particular natural form then this relationship or pattern can easily be assimilated and digested by human beings, for man from within aspires to become more natural, more blissful and to move nearer to the basic existence. Probably this insight initiated man's search for something called 'Brahman', 'Truth' and 'Order'. This curiosity to find the root cause or the truth behind the observed reality laid the foundation stone of science. The exploratory curiosity, imagination, and hope for something extravagant gave rise to the streams of art and culture. Vastushastra is sometimes described as the art and science for expanding the human horizon. We already have discussed at the beginning of the book, the importance of the helix shape for Vastushastra. Here we touch upon the underlying philosophy.

In the twentieth century, scientists observed that the sacred form which exists, extends and equalises the stream of existence is nothing but a helix or a spiral that is a union of right angle and a sphere. The right angle represents the existence, a thought (*purush*) and the sphere represents the shadow of existence, a sentiment (*prakriti*). This right angle with the entire flow of the sphere as a curvature is the basic order of Nature called a 'sacred cut', the Helix.

In nature, two dissimilar phenomena can have their solution under the principles of helix, with identical mathematical description. Again as viewed from the Indian context, it is the dissimilarity that is *Maya* and it is the unique existence that is *Brahma*. It is said that Nature is a mirror in which we can see ourselves and improve ourselves. Scientists have claimed helix as the natural growth shape. Now we will try to ponder, to observe how Vastushastra has used this divine secret in its basic order to promote a good cosmic living, with bliss for all.

Dynamic Balance and Geometric Symmetry

According to the ancient Indian philosophy and theology, the square embodies the perfect, fundamental form. Both the construction of the altars and the architecture of temples are based on the square as the starting point. All other shapes play a secondary role. The circle, for example, represents a state of flux, the expanding energy from its centre evolving its shape, ultimately culminating in the square. The square on the other hand, symbolises order, stability and the final state of evolving life. It is perfection beyond life and death. It is also postulated that the essence of the square is retained by any *mandala* as long as the area is kept unaltered.

Vastushastra systematically codified these ideas so that the entire human race could utilise practically the knowledge contained therein without actually having to measure and study the minute effects of cosmic forces at work.

As discussed in relation to concepts of *nabhi* and *brahmasthal* in this book, nature displays intricate patterns with perfect order and symmetry in various animate and inanimate objects. In both, organic and inorganic systems, forces acting from within, often in combination with environmental factors decide the different classes of regular shapes these systems will evolve into. Curves and surfaces, conceived and studied purely from mathematical interest, find their expression in a variety of exquisite natural specimens. Growth of a crystal is mediated by evolving a helix to form beautiful symmetrical geometrical shapes. Organic growth by accumulation of matter as in the case of horns, tusks, and shells follow the equiangular or logarithmic spiral pattern. Here the requirement imposed by nature is that, each successive increment of growth be self-similar to its predecessor in shape and relative positioning except that it is a magnified version of the latter. And the mathematical curve, *logarithmic spiral*, is the most suitable form for this purpose.

Formation of geometric structures in nature, in general follows extremisation principle, i.e., minimisation or maximisation of certain factors in natural processes. Some examples which can be easily verified are:

a) Law of reflection of light — light ray taking the *shortest path* in its passage between two points,

b) Fermat's principle pointing towards *minimisation of time* of passage of light between two points located in two different media,

c) Honeycomb structure with its hexagonal symmetry in all planes to evolve into a configuration requiring *least quantity of material* for construction,

d) Soap bubbles taking shape to minimise the work done against force of surface tension, or to evolve into *surfaces of minimal area* with specified boundaries, and

e) Geodesic structure having a curve along which the *distance between two neighbouring points is the least.*

All the above principles, in one way or the other, are reflected in the science of Vastu. Shapes like pentagon, octagon, and circle do represent a geometric symmetry, but not a dynamic symmetry or dynamic balance. On the basis of orientation of North-South magnetic axis, these figures do not represent balanced shapes. As against this, squares and rectangles match their axes with geo-magnetic axis. Hence, one can definitely say that squares and rectangles represent dynamically balanced figures and shapes. As explained in adjoining figures, force-lines of gravitation and magnetism do not form any zigzag or cross pattern in squares and rectangles. The flow of elementary particles through such figures will hardly intersect the network of force-lines. This will lead to a healthy, good and salubrious cosmic environment.

There is logic in preference for the square shape in Vastushastra. In essence, a square does justice to the virtues and qualities of all the eight directions. The square embodies the *Prithvi tatva* (earth element) which in turn symbolises *shabda (*speech*), sparsh (*touch*), roop (*shape*), rasa (*taste*), and *gandha (*smell*), the entities catalysts of worldly pleasures. Vastushastra provides the owner of an abode not only peace and tranquillity of mind, but looks after his bodily comforts also (refer to figs. 5.1, 5.2, 5.3).

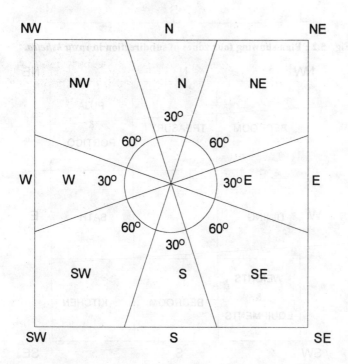

Fig. 5.1 : Plan showing zones of eight directions and degrees.

N
NORTH-WEST ZONE
NORTH-EAST ZONE
W
E
SOUTH-WEST ZONE
SOUTH-EAST ZONE
S

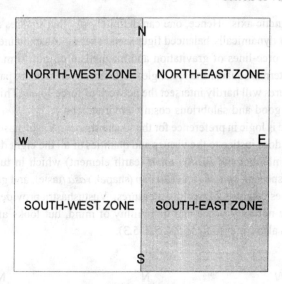

Fig. 5.2 : Plan showing four zones of subdirection in *vastu kshetra.*

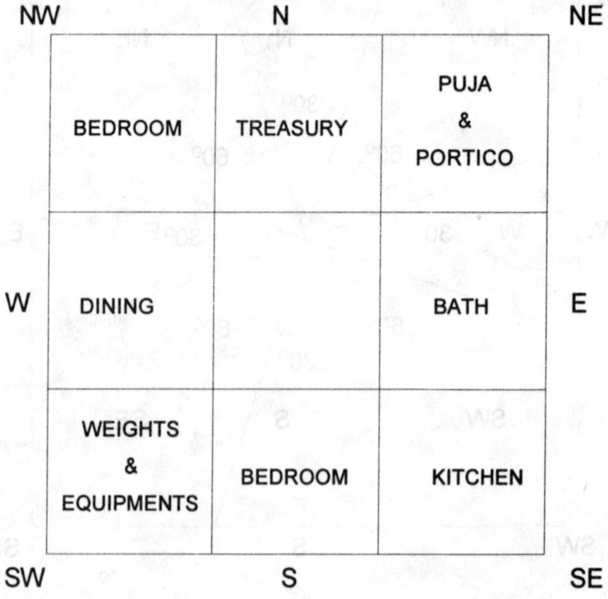

NW
N
NE
BEDROOM
TREASURY
PUJA
&
PORTICO
W
DINING
BATH
E
WEIGHTS
&
EQUIPMENTS
BEDROOM
KITCHEN
SW
S
SE

Fig. 5.3 : Showing the alignments of rooms in respect of directions.

Rectangles with the minor axis along the East-West direction and major axis along the North-South will have the least lateral perimeter exposure to the sun, resulting in cooler and shadow sections, whereas in the reverse case where the minor axis is along the North-South direction, a very large perimeter gets exposed to the sun (fig. 5.4) which is objectionable in Vastushastra.

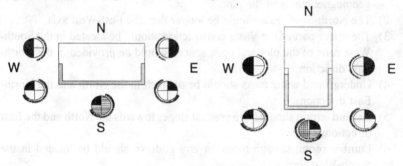

Fig. 5.4 : (A) Exposure to intense solar radation for longer duratio when N-S axis of vastu is shorter than E-W axis (B). Minimum exposure to solar radiation with N-S axis of vastu being longer than E-W axis and matching with the geomagnetic axis.

Any excessively high temperature characteristics create disturbance in magnetic force lines, imparting them with random zigzag pathways leading to cosmic hazards. This is the reason why the *audumber* family trees which are known for heavy absorption of water from soil, are recommended for the South direction which normally is a high temperature zone.

In old structures, the South side walls are found to be thick and wide, and their joints filled with lead plates. It has outstanding characteristics to resist radiation effects. Lead is also used in aprons of X-ray technicians for the same reason. Indeed, the ancient construction techniques reflect a careful and safe approach brought about by deep thinking.

In 1980 U S Environmental Protection Agency (EPA) observed hazardous effects of radiation due to a radioactive gas, radon. Radon evolves through cracks and crevices in rocks and underneath the soil. EPA found that the hazards were serious in buildings which had basements and accordingly recommended filling of basement cavities. This is quite similar to loading of the South-West or the relative unloading of the North-East as suggested in Vastushastra. The similarities in recommendations of the Vastu science and practical applications like the constraints used for fallout structures used in USA are indeed amazing.

Before Planning a Vastu

After analysing the Vastushastra tenets and principles, some ground rules can be formulated for deriving optimum benefits from *Vastu-Vidya* at the planning stage itself.

1) Geometric axis of the Vastu should be aligned to match with the geomagnetic axis of the plot.

2) The North-South axis should be longer than the East-West axis.

3) The major part of the Vastu construction should be located in the South-West zone of the plot and open spaces should be provided in the North-East direction.

4) Underground water tanks should be planned in the North and the North-East directions.

5) Ground terrain should have gradual slopes towards the North and the East directions.

6) Lumber room, storage room, or any godown should be located in the South-West corner.

7) Excavation should commence from the North-East side and move in a clockwise direction towards the South-East side and then onto the South-West direction. Activities like providing a footing for the structure and ground-filling must begin in the South-West.

8) To avoid any ill-effects of the neighbouring Vastu and its domain, it is advisable to complete the construction of the entire compound wall before commencing any other construction activity. The South and the West side compounds should be of stone construction, solid and heavy, and with sufficient height.

9) Soil-analysis should be carried out. The soil not having requisite characteristics as per the Vastushastra should not be used for ground-filling. Good quality soil should be procured from elsewhere for this purpose.

10) A bore-well or a constructed well for a water source should be located in the North or the North-East directions.

11) The South side walls should not have any door or window openings. The wall in this direction should be either an 18 inch (45 cm)-thick construction or a double wall with cavity in-between.

12) Maximum possible number of doors, windows and ventillators should be provided in the North, North-East, and East directions.

13) In the same house, differential levels for internal rooms are not advisable.

14) Basements and cellars should be avoided.

15) Roofs, if provided, should have slopes towards the East, the North-East, and the North directions.

16) Roofs slanting towards the South and the West directions are not advisable.

17) If possible, an additional room or a floor should be constructed on the South-West side.

18) Extra height should be allowed for parapet walls on the South and the West sides.

19) The South-West plinth level should be 9 inches (22.5 cm) higher than the other plinth levels and the planned ground slopes towards the North and East directions should be taken into consideration before determining the other construction levels.

20) *Audumber* family trees should be planted on the South border, while the West side could have *nilgiri* (eucalyptus) trees or medicinal, herbal, and aromatic plants and bushes.

21) The North and the East sides should be provided with open spaces for free air circulation.

22) In cases where the neighbouring plot includes a water-body or pond on its North-East side, the height of the compound wall on the South-West side of one's own plot should be raised sufficiently to make the South-West side extra massive. This provision can be made at the landscaping stage itself.

23) It is considered profitable to purchase additional adjoining land on the North, North-East, and East sides. On no account should any land be acquired on the South or West sides, once a house has been constructed on a plot.

24) In the construction of the structure proper, uneven shapes, fancy windows and unwarranted cantilever projections should strictly be avoided.

25) In ownership flats, options for prior planning are limited. Hence, the Vastu should be made healthy and full of vitality through external means. Selection of a painting scheme for the flat based on the *Shri Ranga Chakra* in such cases proves very helpful.

26) Light-weight items should be placed in the North and the East directions, while rigid and heavy things should be located in the South and the West. This principle is applicable not only to the entire Vastu, but to individual rooms also.

27) If the East side is blocked on any account, additional windows should be provided in the North direction. If possible, the sunlight should be beamed in from the East direction by making use of some sort of reflector mechanism.

28) The North, North-East, and East side walls should be decorated preferably with photographic frames or paintings of goddesses and wallpapers with natural scenery, etc.

29) The North, North-East and East side walls should be painted with bright glossy colours, while the painting scheme for the West and South side walls could use dull, matt-finish type colours.
30) Toilets should be located in the South and the West.
31) A Vastu with 100 per cent matching characteristics and performance as espoused in Vastushastra is an idealistic condition. In practice, it is decidedly necessary or sometimes, even sufficient to achieve a minimum of 50 per cent to 60 per cent of the characterisics of the ideal conditions in a Vastu.
32) The overhead tank should be on the West side. A tank on the North or the East side is also permissible. But, underground or ground level water should never be stored in the West or the South-West directions.
33) One should sleep with one's head pointing towards the West or the South direction. Beds should be arranged accordingly.
34) The puja-room (prayer room) should be planned in such a manner that the back of the goddesses should touch the East side wall, with the person facing the East direction while performing the puja.
35) Multi-coloured fancy lamps should be fixed on the North and the East walls, specifically avoiding the South side surfaces.
36) If possible, the Vastu should be extended by 4-5 ft (1.5 mtrs) in the North-East direction to ensure the North-East directional bliss for the household or a shop.

Vastu *Rachana* (Layout of a House)

A Vastu planned with geometric and magnetic axes of the Vastu parallel and unidirectional does not have to face many of the *vastudoshas*, as these defects are automatically removed because of the Vastu orientation. For a proper alignment with the magnetic axis, the plan of a Vastu, sometimes, has to be rotated slightly with respect to the plot orientation. This concept looks ungainly on the face of it, but it is possible to create an excellent and aesthetically pleasant Vastu just by some simple landscaping and making use of remnant triangular open spaces for additional light.

In order to make South and West sides massive, the side margin available on the South-West side of the plot should be raised by 4-5 ft (1.5 mtrs). This facilitates the process of achieving inclined sloping levels on the North and the East sides. To make use of artificial differential levels, the South-West side should be made heavy and the North-East light weight, while keeping the South-East and North-East sides at relatively higher levels.

Wherever possible, the doors and windows should have dimensions in the *Golden Ratio* of 1:1.618 or 1:1.5, which proves beneficial to the Vastu. Whatever the direction of the approach road to the plot, it is advisable to plan the Vastu in the South and West zones of the plot, for proper energy flow. After all, Vastushastra essence lies in creating pathways for maintaining the correct cosmic energy flow through a Vastu.

Centre of Energy Balance

The centre of energy balance is located at the origin of a logarithmic helix fitted in a rectangle with sides having proportionate *Golden Ratio* of 1:1.618. The concepts behind the *helix* and the *Golden Ratio*, have been illustrated in the accompanying diagrams (figs. 5.5A, 5.5B).

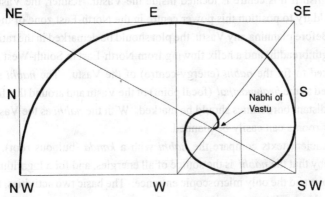

Fig. 5.5.A : Plotting the *nabhi* of Vastu through helix and golden ratio.

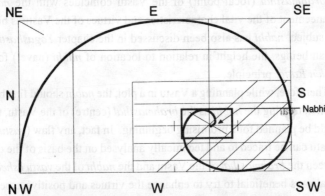

Fig. 5.5.b : Helix in a *vastu kshetra* as per Vastu principles to achieve energy-matter balance. Vastu should be located in the South-West zone.

The idea of constructing a building in the South-West zone implies arranging of the centre of energy balance in the actual building area. This centre is possibly the *nabhi* of *vastu kshetra* (focal point of a plot) as defined in the ancient texts and it is the source of all cosmic energies. The centre is confined to the Vastu by constructing the Vastu in the South-West zone. Here, we are trying to correlate the old doctrine or traditional concepts about *nabhi* with the modern concept of *Golden Ratio*.

A new procedure to locate this power centre, amalgamating the traditional theory of Vastu and modern insight into the *Golden Ratio* is described in the following passages. The effects of most of the *vastudoshas* automatically diminish if this centre is located inside the Vastu. Rather, the Vastu experts should try to position this power centre in the North-East zone of the Vastu.

Before planning any Vastu, the plot should be demarked in the ratio 1:1.618 (length:breadth) and a helix flowing from North-East to South-West should be marked to fix the *nabhi* (energy-centre) of the Vastu. The *nabhi* should be treated as the *brahmasthal* (focal point) of the Vastu and around this focal point equidistant borderlines should be marked. With the *nabhi* as the Vastu centre, other rooms can easily be planned.

Ancient texts compare the *nabhi* with a *kanda* (bulbous root), meaning thereby that the *nabhi* is the source of all energies, and for a logarithmic helix, it is one and the only microscopic entrance. The basic two activities, breathing of the Vastu plot and manifestation of energy, are centred around the *nabhi*. If the *brahmasthal* (focal point) of the Vastu coincides with the *nabhi*, then enhancement of the vital characteristics and virtues of the Vastu is but natural. The subject *nabhi* has also been discussed in the chapter *Yogashastra*. In the human beings, the height in relation to location of *nabhi* (navel) follows the *Golden Ratio* principle.

Therefore, while planning a Vastu in a plot, the *nabhi* should first be located, and then treating the *nabhi* as the *brahmasthal* (centre) of the Vastu, the layout should be planned for a promising beginning. In fact, any flaw (*vastudosha*) in a Vastu can be traced to and technically analysed on the basis of the difference between the *brahmasthal* of the Vastu and the *nabhi* of the *vastu kshetra* (plot). It is always beneficial to try to enhance the virtues and positive aspects of the Vastu by noting this difference in relation to the directional aspects and the degree of influence of the *panch-maha-bhutas* (five basic elements).

If the North-East, North and East sides of the plot are provided with sloping terrain and then the massiveness is increased systematically from South-East to South-West, with a gradual rise towards the South-West and slope towards the North-East, then the *nabhi* of such a plot acts as the centre of all the energies emerging from the interior of the earth and other cosmic energies. This results in the creation of an envelope of life-sustaining energy vibrations around the entire Vastu.

The relationship between various types of *vastu kshetras* (plots) and the methods for establishing the proportionate *nabhi* is illustrated in the following examples.

Establishing the Nabhi of a Vastu
PLOT SIZE : 80 ft X 60 ft (approx. 24.4 m X 18.3 m)

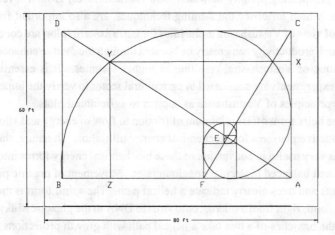

Fig. 5.6 : Geometric construction for locating the *nabhi* of a Vastu.

1) Set aside the side margin on the South and West sides and construct a rectangle ABCD with AC:AB in the ratio of 1:1.618.
2) The logarithmic helix should commence from the point 'D'.
3) The point 'E' is the *mukh* (mouth or inlet) of the helix, and is denoted as the *nabhi* of the plot. The fact that the axes CEF and DEA intersect each other in the *Golden Ratio* points to the correctness of the method adopted for marking the *nabhi*.

After establishing EH:EG and EN:EM in the *Golden Ratio*, the end-points of the Vastu should be marked as WXYZ. This method of first marking the *nabhi* and then fixing the location of the Vastu in a *vastu kshetra* (plot) ensures compliance to most of the edicts of the Vastushastra for bestowing the necessary virtues and excellence on the Vastu being constructed.

Agriculture and Vastushastra

The close relationship between biochemical energy and the tenets of Vastushastra is one of the main themes of this book.

Cultivation of agricultural produce like vegetables, fruits, flowers, mushrooms, etc., is governed by biological processes and can greatly benefit from the insight and practices of Vastushastra. There are inherent advantages in applying principles of Vastushastra for a *vastu kshetra* (plot) to a plot utilised for agricultural purposes. Factors like solar energy and radiation, shadow region, water prospecting, quality of water, soil characteristics, ground levels, plot shapes which influence the farming techniques, are also important from the point of view of Vastushastra as the rules for *vastu kshetra* (plot) are concerned.

Land productivity can greatly be boosted through the 'virtue enhancement' technique of Vastushastra, resulting in higher incomes. It is essential that some experiments are conducted in agricultural sector to verify the importance of the principles of Vastushastra as applied to agricultural plots.

The helix form offers minimum of friction to flow of energy and allows for a productive platform for biochemical energy utilisation. In nature, the helix form is very useful in conversion of these biochemical energy forms into some stable and balanced molecular conglomerates. Movement of organic proteins in plants and trees clearly indicate a helical path. The spiral form is the most active form, right from a microscopic virus to DNA to the gigantic Milky Way. Even the branches of a tree take a helical path with growth projections at 120 degrees with respect to the central stem, spiralling one above the other.

Agriculture is closely associated with soil, water, air, sunlight and space. The Vastushastra rules are inspired by the *panch-maha-bhutas* (five basic elements) manifesting themselves in various living organic forms in nature. As such, agriculture can certainly benefit from effective application of Vastushastra rules. A barrier between the human mind and the intellect can be removed if natural laws get precedence over man-made rules. Since plants and trees adhere to nature in all respects, Vastushastra rules can revolutionalise the whole agricultural scene.

Vastushastra edicts propose slopes towards the North-East, rising level and weight from East to South-East to South with maximum loading in the South-West and then again, gradual lowering of levels from the West to North-West to North. This type of ground layout forms a three-dimensional ascending helix over the agricultural plot, which is nature's way of propagating life-sustaining activities of all the energy sources. This helical form layout essentially adheres to the energy and mass equivalence principle, and the effect of compensating the South-West magnetic tail, southern solar differential temperature zones, magnetic field fluctuations through gravitational mass is automatically achieved for the respective directions.

Vastu Rules for Agriculture

a) Agricultural land should be divided into equal rectangular plots, preferably with breadth:length ratio of 1:1.618. The longer side should be oriented along the North-South axis, while the shorter side along the East-West direction.

b) Electrical power points should be located in the South-East corner.

c) The bunds on the South and West sides should be at a higher level, while those on the East and North sides at a lower level or the ground on these sides should be a flat terrain.

d) One-tenth of the plot on the South-West side should be raised by constructing a solid stone parapet.

e) The ground should have descending slopes towards the North and East sides.

f) Trees should be planted in the South and West directions.

g) Planting of trees in the North and East directions should be avoided.

h) A well should be dug in the North-East, North or East side of the plot.

i) Any shed or a farmhouse on the plot should be constructed in the South-West corner of the plot.

Landscaping as per Vastu Science

Vastudoshas (deficiencies) in the Vastu can be halved just by making some qualitative improvements in the *vastu kshetra* (plot) to endow it with some virtues as pronounced in the Vastushastra. *The Brihad-Samhita* describes a number of trees believed to have benevolent influence on a Vastu. It is definitely an easy task to restructure the ground levels in a plot as per the principles of Vastushastra, provided that a contour plan in the ascending and descending levels of the plot is prepared in advance. The following tenets of Vastushastra govern the landscaping process:

1) Making the South-West side massive and heavy.
2) Loading the South direction.
3) Providing descending slopes towards the North, East and North-East directions.
4. Constructing an underground water tank in the North, East or North-East direction and providing a small water pond or an open water body in one of these directions.
5) Elevating the compound walls on the South, South-West and West directions and ensuring that these are massive and heavy.
6) Constructing the compound walls on the East, North-East and North sides with light weight material and maintaining these at a relatively lower elevation.
7) Locating the electrical power transformer and other electrical power points in the South-East corner.
8) Constructing a cottage in the South-West corner of the plot, with minimum side margins.
9) Planting of *nilgiri* (eucalyptus) trees in the West zone of the plot, along with some varieties of medicinal, herbal and aromatic bushes.

The above tenets allow certain qualitative improvement in a Vastu, endowing it with virtues and purity. A few of the predominant effects are:

a) Interrupting the South *Pingala* current flow.
b) Achieving energy-mass balance through proportionate compensation for geomagnetic and energy disturbances.
c) Augmenting the North *Ida* current flow, bestowing the Vastu with divine bliss.
d) Regulating the excessive Southern zone temperatures through water-vapour emission processes of trees like *nilgiri* (eucalyptus) and *neem* (margosa).
e) Creating a healthy and salubrious atmosphere inside the house through the scent and aroma of herbal plants.
f) Enhancing the quality of the Vastu through beneficial effects of transverse polarisation of sunlight falling on an open water surface.

Planning a Vastu in Plots of Irregular Shape — a Novel Approach

Art of Balancing

The position of a house in a plot, the size and shape of the house are of extreme importance for attaining requisite virtues in a Vastu through balancing of known and unknown forces made possible by proper location of the Vastu in a *vastu kshetra*. Due to harmonious interaction of these forces, the environment inside and outside the house benefits from a type of cosmic energy envelope.

These ancient concepts are traced to the *nabhi* of the plot which is assumed to be the reservoir and source of all energy. Locating the *nabhi* of the plot and relocating its position at the *brahmasthal* (central zone) should be the basic approach of an architect while planning a Vastu. In Hindu mythology the Brahma position is sourced to the *nabhi* of the God of Creation, Lord Vishnu. The similarity of concepts is rather striking and the underlying truth can be applied for attaining harmony in a house by positioning the source of all energies at the central zone of the house. While locating the energy centre in the plot proper, the shape of the plot may suitably be trimmed to achieve a rectangle with the *Golden Ratio* 1:1.618 which will automatically reshape the plot to provide more open spaces in the North and East directions. An exact geometric construction has been described elsewhere in the book for determining the energy centre.

In the art of balancing, we concentrate on simulating effects of extensions and additions of various directions by subtracting or deleting masses, heights or loads while planning a house. A good, balanced posture of a house in a plot bestowing divine bliss on the household can be planned by giving due consideration to the effective influence of each direction.

We will discuss here some cases involving irregular plot shapes and remedial measures to remove the *vastudoshas*.

1) Elevate the South-East and South-West plinth sides.
2) Construct additional floors on the South-East and South-West sides, simultaneously.
3) Add heavy gravitational mass to the shaded directions.
4) Find percentage areas of 'aba1' and 'c1c2c3d'. Compare this percentage with the heavy mass in the plinth or the floors.
5) Extended direction means reduced stress concentration requiring reduced matter content.

CASE 1

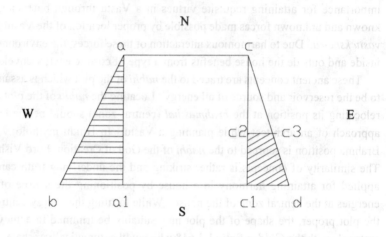

Fig. 5.7 : Trapezoid plot with excess length on the South side.

6) If the plot has extended North, North-East or East directions, the percentage deduction by means of water-bodies, extra slope towards these directions in landscaping, or providing basements in the North, North-East or East directions, or lowering the gravitational mass compared to the South, South-West or West directions are some of the remedial measures.

7) Additional length on the South side and narrowing of the North side require the usual treatment of normal gravitational mass on the South side and maximum open spaces on the North side.

8) In the above case, it is better to locate the building in the central zone of the South boundary instead of the South-West zone which merely adds qualities of relative excess North zone.

Creating more and more terraces on the North side is the basis of planning for this case. The right geometric construction to deal with such problems is found by allowing maximum terrace space in the North direction.

CASE 2

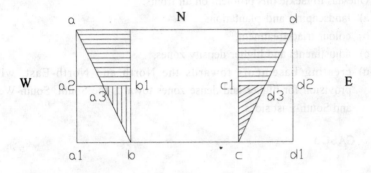

Fig. 5.8: Plot 'abcd' with excess North and reduced South.

The following are the plus and minus points for this plot:
  a) additional North-East,
  b) reduced South-East,
  c) reduced South-West,
  d) additional North-West,
  e) additional West and East,
  f) additional North, and
  g) reduced South.

The net result is excessive stress concentration towards the South due to coagulation of magnetic force lines from extended North region getting focussed on a small width of South region. If the South, South-East and South-West are treated properly, the problem can easily be solved.

1) Calculate the lost South-West and South-East areas 'a₁a₂a₃b' and 'd₁d₂d₃c'.

2) Find the percentage of area lost. Since the loss is on the South-West and South-East sides, it must be compensated through additional *gurutwa* (gravitational mass) on available areas of South-West and South-East, i.e., 'a₃b₁c' and 'd₃c₁c' in proportion to the percentage loss.

3) Additional *gurutwa* is required in plinth levels as well as in floor levels for such critical cases.

4) Compensating for the South-West, South, and South-East area losses through *gurutwa* in a Vastu demands a careful approach, as it can turn out to be a limited case of failure as regards stress concentration.

5) One has to tackle this problem on all fronts:
   a) landscaping and plantations,
   b) colour triad treatment,
   c) adjustments and higher density zones,
   d) creating basements towards the North and North-East, with provision for higher and dense zones towards the South, South-West and South-East sides.

CASE 3

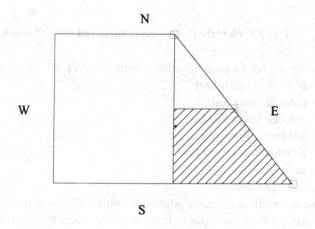

Fig. 5.9: Plot with reduced North and additional South-East sides.

This type of plot is analysed as having the following characteristics:
(a) reduced North, (b) extended South, (c) balanced West, (d) extended East, (e) additional South-East, and (f) loss in North-East.

1) Extended South implies reduced stress concentration, thereby allowing normal loading on the South side.

2) There is a need to create extended South-East zone by adding load on the South-East side. This can be achieved by raising the South-East plinth level or adding an extra floor in the South-East zone.

3) Reduced North needs the following line of treatment:
   a) Place some water source in the North zone.
   b) Construct basements on the North side.
   c) Arrange the roofs in such a manner that these gradually slope towards the North.

4) To reduce the effects of excessive South-East, add some water body in the South-East so that the *Agni tatva* (fire element) associated with this direction can be counter-balanced. But this type of remedy is contradictory to the traditional and classical line of thinking.

5) Availability of excess South-East zone permits the building alignment to be shifted to the South-East corner to match the overall centre of construction with the shifted centre of energy of the entire plot.

We have seen in the above examples that it is not really necessary to discard an irregularly shaped plot of land and that such plots can effectively be put to use through some imaginative reconstruction based on sound understanding of Vastu principles. Beneficial remedial measures are available in Vastushastra for most of the complicated cases.

6

VASTUSHASTRA AND OTHER BUILDING DESIGN TECHNIQUES

The European or the Western art and architecture is basically governed by the three basic principles : the Law of Harmony, the Law of Contrast, and the Law of Balance. Relations between harmony, contrast, and balance are then established either according to the principle of coherence (logical relations) or according to the principle of rhythm (relations based on aesthetics). Further, it is also assumed that any two entities, in general, can be interrelated logically as well as aesthetically. The above principles are based on the adage "art for art's sake". It is quite possible that examples can be found in European architecture having something in common with dwellings built according to edicts of Vastushastra in terms of location of structure, foundation, window openings and open spaces — just as a matter of coincidence, rather than any well-grasped techniques of Vastu science.

The Eastern architecture (Indian, Egyptian and Chinese) on the other hand reflects the inborn urge for harmony with nature and the pre-ordained unity of the soul with the cosmos. Egypt in its period of glory had great structures like the pyramids, China had its own Feng Shui technique for homes and commercial establishments, and in India the building techniques were enshrined in the Vastushastra.

Vastushastra lays down construction norms similar to the building codes by modern-day municipal and other regulatory authorities. These norms were in terms of symbols and mystic religious tenets, so that a God-fearing society could accept these in its ritualistic form. In different regions of India the practice of Vastushastra shows subtle variations to suit local geography, climate and socio-cultural ethos. Vastushastra extracts the finest aspects of art, astronomy, astrology, ayurveda, yogashastra, biology, chemistry and physics to project itself as a super science. It tries to understand the minutest influence of the sun, the moon, the stars, the planets, the geomagnetic field, the earth's atmosphere, wind direction, gravitational force, electromagnetic radiation on living organisms and human life and gives feasible solutions on site selection, and establishes a logical sequence of house-building activities like s. point, excavation, soil selection, material selection, wall thickne   , orientation and dimensions of rooms, decoration, etc.

Vastushastra covers the entire building science along with topics like solid testing techniques, orientation, measurement and proportion, divination, astrology, ceremonies associated with the construction of buildings. This book has dwelt on some of these topics, but further research needs to be undertaken to clarify and evaluate these various aspects of Vastushastra.

Vastushastra and Geomancy

Prabhat Poddar, an architect associated with the Sri Aurobindo Institute of Applied Scientific Research in Pondicherry, in his paper published in *Architecture and Design* in 1991, wrote that 'Vastu' studied the effects of the natural and built environment on the human system through geomancy or the divination skills. A recent development in this field is the science of geobiology, which uses simple instruments like 'Lecher Antenna', 'Lobe Antenna' and 'Biometer' to measure subtle energies being emitted by the earth, trees, living organisms, inanimate objects, etc.

Biometer was a scale developed by Antoine Bovis and his colleague Andre Simonton to measure various energy fields existing around us. As a matter of convention, these fields are measured in units of 'Bovis'. Measurements carried out by European and Indian scientists have yielded the following values:

Table 6.1: Measured Values of Bio-energy for Humans and Religious Symbols

Healthy human being	(+) 6500 Bovis
Different *chakras* in the body	(+) 6500 to 16000 Bovis
Ringing of church bells	(+) 11000 Bovis
Call from East-facing mosque	(+) 12000 Bovis
Garbhagriha in Tibetan temples	(+) 14000 Bovis
Tibetan prayer wheel	(+) 12000 to 16000 Bovis
Buddhist stupa	(+) 12000 Bovis
Hindu swastika (any size)	(+) 10 lakh Bovis (positive)
Hindu swastika (reverse direction)	(-) 10 lakh Bovis (negative)
Hitler's swastika (45 degree tilt)	(+) 1000 Bovis
Red flower	(+) 6500 Bovis
Fire (any type, any form, any size)	infinite positive energy
Sandstone, marble, etc.	high positive energy
Granite, quartz and some gemstones	negative energy

We once again find that the *shubh* (auspicious) symbols like 'swastika' utilised in Vastushastra practice have some definite purpose like minimising the sources of negative energy and creating an environment full of positive energy useful for the body and the mind.

As proposed by Dr Ernst Hartmann in 1970 and later on experimentally confirmed by some scientists, energy lines emerging from the earth's surface have been observed forming a grid all around the earth. These energy lines are oriented magnetically in the North-South and the East-West direction and are termed as 'Bio-Electro-Magnetic' (BEM) fields. Since each body cell can act like a radio receiver with its own vibratory fundamental frequency, these fields are known to affect the human mind and body, especially at the place of work and sleep where the body remains stationary for a long period of time. Poddar has found that some Himalayan monasteries oriented the cells for monks within the BEM grids, a neutral zone. This interplay of energies is evident in the basic design of Vastu Purush Mandal, if the symbols and images of God incorporated therein are interpreted in a logical manner. In a sense the concept of B E M grid may be a step in the right direction for comprehensive study of the super science, Vastushastra.

Vastushastra Remedial Measures — a Methodology
In an article in *Scientific American,* Kevin N. Lewis says:From experimental studies as well as analysis of air-raid casualties during the Second World War, it has been established that the human body is much more resistant to the direct impact of a bomb blast than is, say, the wall of a building. But as far as nuclear explosion or natural background radiation is concerned, the resistance of the human frame is purely of academic interest.

In a wider sense, the human body and mind need special protection from the invisible energy fields of nuclear radiation, thermal radiation and, in general, destructive electromagnetic radiation. The immediate benefit of Vastushastra lies in the fact that it lays down guidelines which are helpful in designing human dwellings or houses which minimise the stress levels on human body resulting from gravitational, thermal and electromagnetic radiations acting individually or in combination.

In his book *The Body in Question*, Jonathan Miller says : In the detection of a disease in the human body the trio of findings, feelings and failings are generally employed. Findings or discoveries like change in complexion, swelling, shrinkage are noticeable to everyone. Feelings like pricks, stabs, aches and pains are subjective experiences. But, failure to perform or errors in performance by a part of a body is generally noticed by external observer while the subject, as in a case involving brain injury, may or may not be aware of the shortcoming.

Vastushastra assumes a Vastu to be a living soul (*Vastu-Purush*) with all the associated life-sustaining activities and diseases (*vastudoshas*). In finding remedy on any particular *vastudosha*, we again have to utilise the framework of *findings, feelings* and *failures* for a proper diagnosis. Without understanding the implications of the guidelines elaborated in Vastushastra, attempting structural alterations based on some preconceived notions or half-baked knowledge through hearsay can sometimes prove detrimental to the Vastu and its occupants. It is advisable to consult experts in the field for solving Vastu-related problems. Computer generated solutions can be employed only if the programme is elaborate, thorough, and makes use of all the possible variables defined by the Vastushastra. But, all said and done, the gut-feeling of a Vastu expert during his visit to a site many a time proves more decisive than the commonly employed thumb-rules.

Vastushastra and Feng-Shui

It is imperative that two of the well-kown Eastern design methods–Feng-Shui (China) and Vastushastra (India) – are understood in a proper perspective, as both these disciplines in their own ways define the relationship between man and the cosmos. Though French translations of *Maana Saara* and *Maya Saara* (comprehensive books on Vastushastra) were available early this century, these have merely served as academic reference books and no concerted efforts were made to present Vastushastra ideas to general international readership. In contrast, a score of well-designed books on Feng-Shui are available in book-shops across Europe and America. The current scenario indicates that the Feng-Shui technique has found some ardent followers outside China in Taiwan, Hong Kong, Singapore, Europe and the USA, while the world at large is yet to be exposed to the all-encompassing Vastushastra which is indeed unfortunate as Vastushastra principles can find universal application.

In Chinese language Feng means wind and Shui means water, implying thereby that the technique involves balancing of the cosmic element water and the cosmic quality 'wind' in a system to achieve harmony with the cosmic forces. Feng-Shui endows a house or a structure with Qi, the cosmic breath, which must have a free passage in the world governed by Yin-Yang (the male and the female principles) forces.

Vastushastra has clear-cut definitions — *Vastu* means abode or a house and *shastra* means science or technology, i.e., it is the scientific method of house construction. Vastushastra considers a house to be a living soul, the *Vastu-Purush*, having *Prana* (life sustaining force) and breathing being governed by the *Suryanadi* and the *Chandranadi* which have relevance to directional aspects. It is interesting to note that the ancient Chinese Feng-Shui scripts denote water, fire, wood, gold, and earth as the basic five elements forming the entire universe with 'wind' as the special quality attainable by these elements. Vastushastra and the Vedic scriptures stress that every living and non-living entity, and for that matter the entire world, is created out of the *panch-maha-bhutas* — earth, water, fire, wind and ether. The *akash tatva* loosely translated as 'ether' is considered the most important element in this system, as every possible transformation from one element to the other has to be routed through *akash tatva* only.

Geomancy or the technique of mapping the energy lines said to be emerging out of the earth, plays an important role in Feng-Shui, for selection of site for construction purposes. While physical topography of the location decides the site, the actual directions are determined through *Luopan,* a magnetic compass indicating   different characteristics through 36 rings marked on the dial. Vastushastra has its own system of *vastu-chakras,* which is used in conjunction with Astrology, Astronomy and Yogashastra for site-selection, and a magnetic compass decides the directional aspect. Sometimes gut-feeling of the Vastushastra expert visiting the site is an overriding factor. Interestingly, both the systems insist on North-South orientation for a structure.

Feng-Shui considers a land having reddish or yellowish soil as a good geomantic land. Vastushastra recommends a land with white and yellow-coloured soil for house construction. Red-coloured soil is sometimes tolerated in Vastushastra, but a site with black soil is proscribed for construction purposes as such lands are prone to water-logging problems, and act as thermal reservoirs which trap solar heat during daytime and emit this heat during the night — a kind of environmental pollution.

As far as the actual structure is concerned, Feng-Shui has its preferred dimensions of 43/8 cms and 43 cms or their multiples for designing rooms, doors, windows, etc. Vastushstra follows the *Golden-Ratio* (rectangular sides in the ratio of 1:1.618 or 1:1.5) principle for designing of entrances, doors, windows, etc., with square shape as the ideal shape for the house.

Feng-Shui insists that a body of water should flow in front of the main entrance of the house for beneficial influence of cosmic forces on the household. There is no preferred direction of water-flow as Feng-Shui allows positioning of the main entrance in either North or East or South or West directions, depending on the birth-year of the owner of the house. Vastushastra on the other hand considers water-flow in the direction North-East to the Vastu as a beneficial factor with lunar-shaped (*chandrakar*) North-East directional flow as a pointer to fame and prosperity.

As mentioned above, the horoscope and the birth-year of the owner determine the direction of the main entrance in Feng-Shui technique, while in Vastushastra the favourable directions are the North and the East, with other directions sometimes allowed, based on the horoscope of the owner and topography of the plot.

A major discrepancy in both these disciplines pertains to the direction of windows or ventilator openings. Feng-Shui brands the North as an 'evil' direction for window openings and prefers the South direction. In contrast, Vastushastra dictates that the windows should be positioned in the North, the East or the North-East directions only. The Feng-Shui concept attempts to offer the households protection against yellow dust and sand which the Chinese mainland receives from the deserts situated on the North border of that country. Vastushastra follows scientific logic in selection of the window directions, in the sense that it considers the beneficial effects of early morning sunlight and the benign geomagnetic flux in choosing the directions.

Location and design of rooms in Feng-Shui are based on the traditional *Le-Shu* grid of nine squares which assigns different directions for hall, study, bedroom, kitchen, attic, etc. In Vastushastra, the location of living room, *puja* room, bedroom, kitchen are designated in the Vastu Purush Mandal, consisting of nine squares as influenced by the journey of the sun in its various phases (*aditya, agni, yama,* etc.) throughout the day. The scientific insight behind the design of Vastu Purush Mandal has been discussed elsewhere in this book.

There is no restriction on location or direction of the kitchen inside a house in Feng-Shui designs, provided that the stove faces the South or the East directions. Vastushastra prefers South-East corner for location of the kitchen, and sometimes permits other directions, except the North-East, subject to the condition that the stove is placed in the South-East corner of the kitchen and the person cooking the meals faces the East direction. As far as sleeping arrangements are concerned, Vastushastra advises that the head should preferably be located towards the South or else towards the East while sleeping. This logic is based on the study of minute effects of geomagnetic flux lines on the human mind and body. Feng-Shui lays down similar tenets, but prefers body orientation for sleeping slightly off-axis from the actual North-South or East-West directions with no preferences as far as orientation of head. A sloping roof over a bedroom is considered evil by Feng-Shui, while roofs on any rooms sloping towards the South, the West or the South-West are to be avoided as per Vastushastra principles.

Feng-Shui considers the North direction as a door to spirituality, but surprisingly brands the North-East as a door to evil. Vastushastra symbolism, which is based on scientific considerations like transition phases of the sun and solar radiation flux, says that the North is governed by Kuber, the Lord of Wealth, and the North-East is governed by Ish, the Lord Supreme. Feng-Shui allots the symbol 'circle' to the heaven and 'square' to the earth and bestows superiority to round objects. Vastushastra lays down that the square shape which represents the element 'earth' is a dynamically balanced shape, while a round shape which represents 'wind' is dynamically unstable. The stability and reliability of the square and rectangular objects has been separately discussed elsewhere in this book.

The remedial actions in Feng-Shui, rely on improving 'Qi', the cosmic breath of a house. Vastushastra improves the 'guna' (virtues) of a Vastu by employing 'Vastu-Chakras' (*Avakahada Chakra, Shri Ranga Chakra, Dwar Parinivesh Phal,* etc.) after assessing the deficiencies of a Vastu in relation to the 'Vastu Purush Mandal'.

It is quite apparent that Vastushastra, though shrouded in mystery and symbolism, follows certain scientific principles acceptable to the modern world and has universal applications. Techniques like Feng-Shui, based more or less on local geographic considerations and traditions, may virtually be ineffective when employed beyond the Chinese mainland.

Vastushastra and Pyramids

Pyramids and pyramid-like structures have been a strong identity of the ancient Egyptian and Mayan cultures, though pyramids have also been discovered in China, Cambodia, India, Siberia, Mexico and some parts of South America and Central America. The purpose of these huge edifices is not very clear, though there are clues available that the Egyptian pyramids served as burial chambers for 'Pharaohs', the kings and the Mayan pyramids were used for religious rituals. The rulers of those eras considered proper and orderly contact with the heavenly powers as an essential condition for economic and political well-being. The monumental architecture of these structures is a pointer to this divine urge.

As understood in solid geometry, the pyramid is a structure with a polygonal base with sloping sides meeting at an apex point. Egyptian pyramids are marked by a solid square base and a definite apex point, Mayan pyramids exhibit square or pentagonal base and the sloping sides terminating into a flatted top, rather than an apex. The Great Pyramid of Gizeh is considered mathematically and geometrically, the most perfect structure.

Some research scientists in Egyptology believe that the pyramids, though at present located in a desert, were in fact built in a river (now extinct), and served as artificial rain-making machines. The current interest in pyramid technology stems from discoveries reported all over the world that pyramid-like structures help in healthy growth of plants placed inside, and act as rejuvenators for the human body and mind. Exprimenters are trying to establish the nature of mysterious energy fields inside a pyramid and the actual energy flow from the base to the apex, with the assumption that pyramids serve as energy field resonators or generators of energy.

The common link between the Vastushastra principles and the logical thinking that conceived the idea of a pyramid lies in the field of channellising the cosmic energy flow for some constructive purpose. But, it must be remembered that pyramids were constructed for the benefit of the Pharaohs and their souls, while Vastushastra strives for betterment of the entire mankind.

Vastushastra successfully uses pyramids, pyramidal structures (fig. 6.1) and pyramidal forms to offset *vastudoshas* related to the Southern entrance and deficiencies in the West direction of a house. Pyramids of materials like grass, bamboo, wood are used as sources of organic energy to confine the chaotic inorganic energy (refer to discussion on *Jaivic* and *Pranic Urja* and Vastu Purush Mandal in Chapter 4).

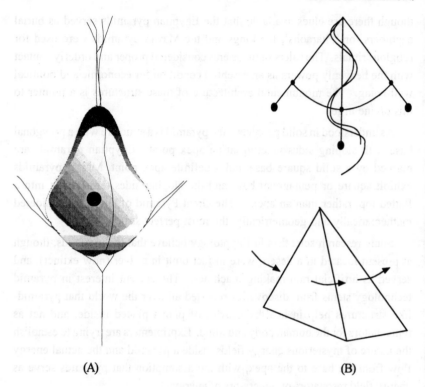

(A)   (B)

Fig.6.1 :   **Pyramidal structures of interest (a) Neuron having pyramidal form (b) Pendulum motion of *rudraksh* transformed into gyral motion at the apex of a pyramid.**

Vastushastra and Modern Architecture

Modern architecture as taught in India borrows heavily from the West European architecture which has at its base total utilitarian view of life, and superficially draws sustenance from concepts like balance, harmony, rhythm, form, shape, proportion, functional utility, efficiency and beauty. These concepts are valid in Vastushastra also, but the inspirations differ. While Vastushastra attempts to design dwellings which are beneficial to the body and mind of the dweller, modern architecture sometimes gets so much obsessed with ideas like economy, lifestyle, function, and efficiency that it almost forgets the inherent psychological needs like peace and tranquillity of a human being occupying the structure. Sometimes, the hands of an architect are forced because of professional compulsions like satisfying the demands of builders and developers. The individuality in architectural creations, visible in earlier times, has in recent times been lost to problems associated with group or mass housing techniques.

In Vastushastra as well as modern architecture, shapes like the square and the rectangle indicate safety, completeness and stability. But the shapes in the nature of triangle, indicative of security and rounded shapes representing grace and progress in modern architecture are avoided in Vastushastra. Modern architecture, though outwardly elegant, is yet to imbibe the smooth way in which Vastushastra has found balance between symmetry and asymmetry in designing structures.

With architectural students actively seeking exposure to the traditional Vastushstra and concepts like cosmic energy flow, the practice of modern architecture is bound to undergo substantial changes. An expert in Vastushastra is supposed to know not only architecture, but other disciplines like Yogashastra and Astrology. Indeed there are many practising architects in India who are enthusiastically using concepts from Vastushastra, and cosmic energy flow and analysis in their designs with positive results. Despite the fact that architects are forced by constraints imposed by developers and builders to limit themselves to predetermined design techniques, there definitely is a great appreciation for ancient Vastushastra amongst the architectural fraternity.

7

PRACTICAL VASTUSHASTRA ANALYSIS

Here we will examine a couple of Vastus (dwellings) as located in different types of *vastu ksheiras* (plots) with reference to Vastushastra principles pertaining to qualitative aspects of different directions and building layout.

Analysis of Vastu 'A'

1) *Main entry towards South-West :* This is considered to be one of the worst kinds of *dosha* (defect) in Vastu Science. With stress concentration at its maximum, this zone is completely disturbed. To reduce the bad effects caused by this deficiency, pyramids of organic matter like wood or bamboo are suggested.

2) *Main door is two-leafed :* This effects more openings towards the South and the West, providing access to *Yama Pravah.*

3) *Circular staircase :* Vastushastra prefers staircases to be rectangular so that main axis is along magnetic axis.

4) *North-East cut to building* : The North-East cut to a building hampers the general rectangular shape of building, thus affecting the parallelism between the main axis and the geometric axis.

5) *Kitchen to the South :* The perfect zone for a kitchen is the South-East zone (*Agneya*) which is related to temperatures that are in perfect fusion with activities in the kitchen.

6) *Main entrance to the South-East :* The South-East entry intermingled with bad effects of the South (abode of Yama) causes disharmony and discontent in the house.

At first sight, we may get instinctively overwhelmed by the arrangement of the plan. But after close observation, many faults with reference to Vastu principles are detected.

1) *Toilet to East* : It is a strong *dosha* in Vastu. The East is considered to be a holy zone. Toilets here lead to disturbance of the moral character of a man, thus affecting his family life.

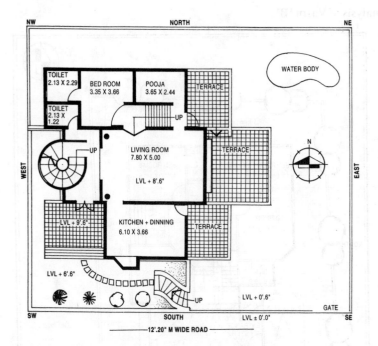

Fig.7.1 : Plan of Vastu 'A'

2) *Bedroom to the South-East* : The South-East being the zone of *Agneya* (fire) leads to all sorts of thermal imbalances. A person residing in this zone is likely to be affected (burnt up from within) by these thermal disturbances. A bedroom to South-East leads to disagreements, court matters, divorce cases, etc.

3) *Wide Opening to the South* : This opening gives way to *Yama Pravah* and *Vish Kau* from the atmosphere. All ventillators acting as sources of light from the South side are placed in the opposite direction to the natural North-South electromagnetic flux. Mythologically this is termed as *Pran* and *Jeev* in opposition, denoting Yama as a symbol to the South in Vastu Purush Mandal. Hence, openings to the West and the South are not advisable. Tilted bay windows can be installed so as to get effective light from the North or the East.

Analysis of Vastu 'B'

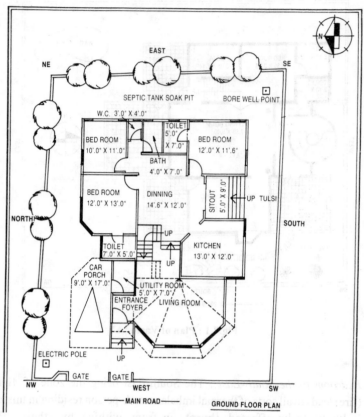

Fig.7.2 : Plan of Vastu 'B'

4) *Kitchen Platform* : The kitchen platform should be oriented such that the user's face is towards the East.

5) *Staircase* : In general, a staicase has to be clockwise while going up.

6) *Main Entrance* : The entrance to the building is from the West. The main entry from the West is not advised in Vastu science. This is considered as a *dosha* in Vastushastra. To reduce bad effects caused by such an entrance, construct pyramids in organic matter such as bamboo or wooden planks. The basic function of these pyramids is to absorb the stresses and concentrate these at a point.

7) If possible, entry from the North or East should be provided.

Analysis of Vastu 'C' & 'D'

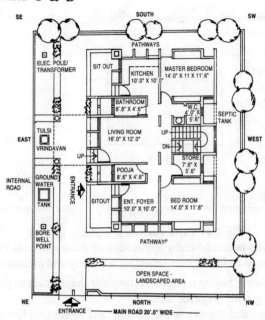

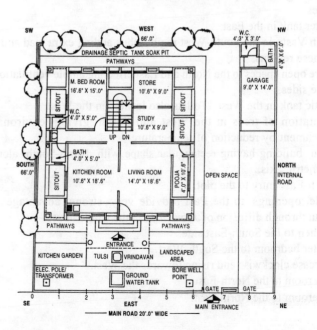

Vastu Analysis of a Plot

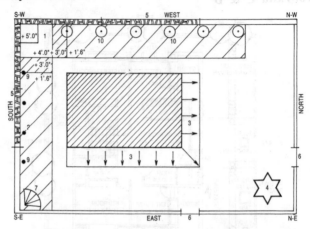

Fig. 7.4 : Vastu analysis of a plot in general.

Below are given points whereby application of these will help in building up a perfect home to reside in, thus reflecting a healthy and pleasant atmosphere.

1) *Vastu kshetra,* having a perfect rectangular shape, leads to geometric axis coinciding with magnetic axis.
2) General ground slopes towards the East and North give low mass to these zones.
3) Water tank in the East.
4) Main Vastu in the South-West region, thus adding extra load and matter to these regions.
5) More open spaces to the North and East effecting ample ventillation from these sides.
6) Septic tank in the West. Toilets also located in the West.
7) Plantation of trees in the West and South giving environmental enrichment by reduction of temperature.
8) Main building having rectangular shape with North-South along the geometric axis.
9) North-East entry to the plot.
10) Wide openings to the East provide very strong advantage to the Vastu through diffusion of *Jaivic urja* in the whole house.
11) Kitchen to the South-East side.
12) Master bedroom to the South-West.
13) Staircase clockwise and rising towards the West.
14) *Puja* room to the North-East.
15) Storeroom to the North-East.

1) Provide heavy pedestal load (*gurutwa load*) in the South-West corner. The South-West zone being the zone of high thermal activity leads to all sorts of disturbances in the aligned magnetic fields of Vastu. A balance of this distubed energy is obtained by heavy loads in this region. These heavy loads absorb the high solar energy and keep the surroundings cool.

2) Provide fillings to the West/South so as to maintain ground slope towards the North and the East.

3) Maintain the main buildings to the South-West corner with elevated plinth. Vastu principles do not admit any void to the South-West zone. The South-West zone being the zone of heavy stress concentration leads to disturbance in the matter and energy which in turn reflect on the consciousness and human intellect.

4) Provide exposed water body with marble finish in the North-East corner. Water exposed to N-E polarises the sunbeams/electromagnetic rays in transverse direction giving eternal non-perishable source of organic energy.

5) Provide heavy compound wall in stone masonry having the following dimensions;

    thick and 7'0" high to South-West corner.

    thick and 5'0" high to West zone.

    thick and 6'0" high to South zone.

6) Provide lightweight compound wall to the North and the East. To match the shape and size and periphery of the *vastu kshetra* with the concept of helix, variational depths/heights/widths of the compound wall are suggested. The helical aligning of the compound wall will equalise the virtues and vices related to directions and sub-directions.

7) Provide main entry to the North or the East.

8) Planting of trees based on *Vruksha-Vichar* is a well defined concept in Vastu analysis. There appears to be a close affiliation between plants and human beings, a relationship that goes far beyond the sharing of chemical substances. Plant trees around the periphery of the property as per details given below:

    a) East   ——   *Kuchla*
    b) North-East   ——   *Khair, Velu*
    c) North   ——   *Pimpal*
    d) North-West   ——   *Jayee*
    e) West   ——   *Arjun*

    f)   South-West   ——   *Nagkeshar*

    g)   South   ——   *Rui*

    h)   South-East   ——   *Moha*

In addition to these, plant *audumber* and *neem* trees on the South side so as to provide a humid environment, thus giving environmental enrichment due to reduction of temperature. Plant medicinal shrubs, *nilgiri* on the West side. The West/North-West is the region of the third basic element *Vayu*. Hence shrubs, medicinal plants, *nilgiri* plantations will give an aroma and bliss based on *Vruksha Vichar* to the entire vessel of the Vastu.

Vastushastra Approach

It is observed that Vastushastra principles have a wide-ranging usage and these can be applied to the analysis of characteristics of not only human abodes, but of public places, human settlements, nations, etc. For this type of exercise, proper understanding of the subject is a must. Superficial application of Vastu principles only complicates matters and results in inaccurate analysis.

India and Vastushastra

It would be interesting to analyse the character of the Indian nation through the Vastushastra insight. Many a pundit avers that everything is wrong with India from the Vastushastra point of view, which is an incorrect proposition resulting from misinterpretation of geology of India (Fig. 7.5) and a strong influence of Western thinking that peace and universal brotherhood are unimportant features compared to material comforts and financial prosperity.

It would be a childish attempt to make predictions on the basis of cosmetic notions like water in the South-West and slope towards the South. For making a correct assessment the following influencing factors have to be studied in detail—balancing of geomagnetic fields, solar thermocouple action, geophysical layout, geological locations of rivers and the seas, mineral deposits and directionwise gravitational distribution and relative density of landmass.

The Indian culture has always projected the highest traditions and values cherished by all mankind, which is the right clue for Vastushastra analysis of India. The following points must be considered for this study:

1)   Himalayas in the North-East (cold region, stable geomagnetic zone).

2)   Natural shape of India (dynamically balanced conditions).

3)   North-South axis longer than East-West axis.

4)   Location of centre of gravity in the central zone of the landmass.

5) The Sahyadri mountains in the West (solid mass of great height).
6) Mineral deposits (gravitational mass).
7) India conforming to the 'Omkar' shape.
8) Geological dissimilarities and multiplicity.
9) Hollow landmass in the South-West blocked by a solid Deccan trap.
10) *Brahmasthal* of India.
11) Slopes towards the Eastern sector.
12) Water-body in the South-East.
13) Lunar-shaped water flow in the Eastern region.

Vastushastra considers the square and the rectangle as the best shapes, as from the point of view of providing side margins and adhering to Vastushastra norms it is convenient to construct a building on such a plot. But, Vastushastra principles need closer examination while applying to a region or a nation, in the same way as any universally applicable forecast needs flexible interpretation of rules sacrosanct in personal horoscopes.

With a little bit of imagination, we can visualise India as having a rhombus form (Fig. 7.5). The North-East, the most critical zone, because of gravitational mass of the mountain ranges, could have been considered deficient from Vastushastra point of view, but for the deep snow covering. The North-East mountain ranges with heights 3,000 metres from the mean sea level have a snow-covering throughout the year. It is an established fact that ice floats on water because of its relative lower density compared to water. Thus, the presence of water and relatively lower gravity in the North-East region of India is definitely beneficial to the entire Indian nation as evidenced by cultural and religious developments through some divine grace. The cold environment also decelerates cosmic rays and radiation particles, reducing their destructive power. The cold region also ensures a geomagnetic zone with undisturbed and stable field lines in the North-East direction of India. All this results in improving Vastu-virtues of the North-East in spite of the presence of the giant Himalayas.

As seen in the map of India, the ill-effects of the hollow region in the South-West due to the Arabian seas is effectively blocked by unfragmented solid rock structure of the Deccan trap. In the Deccan plateau, the South-West part is a highly dense gravitational mass with the land sloping towards the East, a feature considered beneficial in Vastushastra.

Considering the depths of continental shelves on the Western and South-Western coasts of India, it can be inferred that the South-West zone is relatively heavy with respect to the North-East zone because of greater water mass with higher density compared to quantitatively less ice-water mass with lower density in the North-East. A relatively dense and heavy South-West is considered a plus point in Vastushastra. And, on a world scale, compared to the depths of Pacific or Atlantic Oceans, the Arabian Sea is relatively shallow, proving that the fears expressed by some Vastushastra practitioners of an abyss on the South-West border of India are unfounded.

The plateau adjacent to Madhya Pradesh and Uttar Pradesh has a height of approximately 100-300 metres from the mean sea level. This *brahmasthal* of India as per Vastushastra is solid and strong because this territory is in general, a flat tableland. Maximum amount of flowing river water runs through this region. The major rivers of India meander in this terrain in a North to East lunar-shaped flow, a positive aspect as per Vastushastra. Eastward flowing water, descending to the Eastern terrain, and flat equidistant *brahmasthal* are all indicative of freedom for cultural interaction, thinking process, arts and talents along with superior religious values in life, and gallantry with self-control as documented in the history of India.

But due to the presence of deserts and slopes towards the North-West, this freedom has been abused, as evident in the history and the current social scenario in India. Then there is a shortfall in energy required to compensate these for ill-effects due to the presence of water in the South-East direction. As such, India will always be affected by political instability and inadept governance. History tells us that India, the source and fountain of spiritual and religious values for the entire world has always suffered reverses as far as unity and combined strength are concerned. The only redeeming feature is the high degree of tolerance and relatively low degree of violence in society, compared to some other nations because of relatively heavy gravitational mass in the South-West and the divine character of the North-East.

Coming back to the points discussed on religious symbolism and Vastushastra, it is amazing to note the way the symbol of good omen *Omkar* conforms to the map of India. This may foretell development of leadership adhering to spiritual values, to lead India to its glory.

Mantrashastra - Vastushastra - Modern Science
The electromagnetic spectrum consists of visible white light with seven colours from violet to red, long wavelengths from infrared onwards and short wavelengths from ultraviolet and beyond. Vedic literature as also certain Eastern philosophies consider the human body to be consisting of *panch-koshas* (five sheaths) which in turn have correlation with *panch-maha-bhutas* (five basic elements) with symbolic affinity with five deities. Physics describes four states of matter — solid, liquid, gas and plasma. The elementary particles

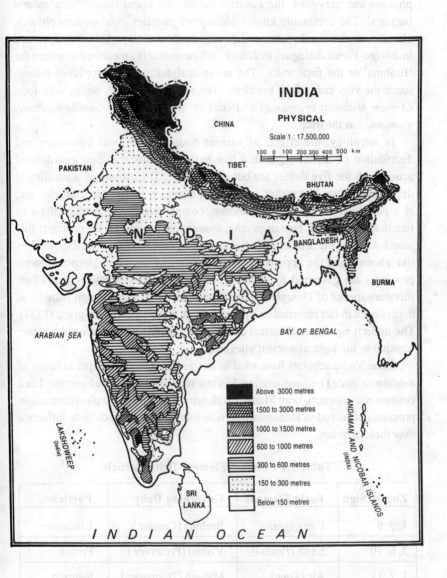

Fig.7.5: Geological features of the Indian landmass.

sics are grouped with increasing masses under five headings — massless p... ons and gravitons, the electron family, the muon family, mesons and baryons. The commonly known elementary particles from modern physics, electron, neutron and proton composing an atom are symbolically discussed in *Bhrigu-Varun* dialogues in *Taittariya Upanishad* in an attempt to search for 'Brahma' or the final truth. The micro-analytic methods employed therein touch the very core of the problem. The self-introspection begins with food *(Annam brahmeti vyanjanat)* and ends in mental bliss *(Anando brahmeti vyanjanat)* as the truth.

In astrology, the effects of various houses in personal horoscope and distribution of zodiac signs into five basic .elements and their coordinated action with the five deities are but astonishing. The actions of scientifically defined quantities like matter, anti-matter, quarks, massless particles, etc., are, at a particular level of understanding, comparable to the fundamentals of functioning of mind, human psyche, thought processes and the concepts like *panch-koshas*. Electromagnetic fields serve as a medium for massless particles like photons and the apparently visible electrochemical and electromagnetic processes are governed by exchange of these massless particles. Buddhist literature speaks of *Thought is matter* and in modern times thought patterns of the brain are in fact recorded on a paper through electro-encephelo-graph (EEG). The underlying electrochemical and electromagnetic processes need a closer scrutiny in the light of ancient allegories.

Some Vedic scholars have tried to interpret mythical concepts in terms of modern science, i.e., associating Vishnu with the concept of proton, Lord Brahma with electron, Lord Mahesh with neutron, etc. The creation/destruction processes observed in elementary particle interactions has a definite influence over these scholars.

Table 7.1 : Zodiac-Element-Deity-Particle

Zodiac Sign	Basic Element	Governing Deity	Particle
1, 5, 9	Fire *(Agni)*	Brahmā (Creator)	Electron
2, 6, 10	Earth *(Prithvi)*	Vishnu (Preserver)	Proton
3, 7, 11	Air *(Vayu)*	Mahesh (Destroyer)	Neutron
4, 8, 12	Water *(Jal)*	Ganesh (Duality)	Ion

Table 7.2 Element-Veda-Energy Form

Basic Element	Thematic Ved	Nature of Hymns
Earth (*Prithvi*)	Rigveda	Vibrations (*Spandan*)
Water (*Jal*)	Yajurveda	Waves (*Valaya*)
Fire (*Agni*)	Atharvaveda	Light (*Prakash*)
Air (*Vayu*)	Samaveda	Sound (*Dhwani*)

The above concepts may have their origin in the realisation that an electron produces light through energy level transition, and molecule formation is possible only through electron bonding, that proton has infinite lifetime, and that a free neutron always decays into an electron and a proton, and that an ion can have either a positive or a negative charge. Vedic literature through its hymns tried to create a particular type of effect on the human body and mind. Rituals and sacrifices apart, these hymns produce synergetic fields for stimulating the microscopic cells and the *panch-koshas* to act in consonance with the five basic elements and the five deities.

Mantrashastra covers the entire gamut of rhythmic recitation to invoke the elements, to bestow the elements with certain virtues and to accentuate their actions. These basic elements with their essence captured in *Dhwanimantras* and *Beejmantras* (hymns) coming to fruition in the five sheaths — physical, vital, emotional, cognitive, super-consciousness as manifested by *anna* (food), *pran* (spirit), *chakshu* (eyes), *kshotra* (ears), and *mana* (mind) — a process necessary for permeating human evolution and developed by ancient seers, is a boon for all mankind. The recitation of hymns on the occasion of rituals like *Vastushanti*, *Udakshanti*, and *Grahashanti* may have some micro-energy transformation effects, which, perhaps, may stand the scrutiny by modern science.

In Vastushastra, the eight directions are correlated with the five basic elements. Excellent Vastu can only result from coordinated action of the best virtues of the five elements. As per the Vedic concepts *Karmendriyas* (five senses of action) and *Jnanendriyas* (five organs of perception) of a man are evolved through and are directly influenced by *panch-maha-bhutas* (five basic elements) which are directly related to a Vastu. The solid foundation of Vastushastra discipline draws its sustenance from the logically perfect solutions it can provide for deficiencies of elements in a Vastu after some detailed examination. Thus, Vastushastra makes use of insights from Vedic hymns, Yogashastra, Astrology and Ayurveda (refer to Table 3.2) to design dwellings that ensure creative development of human body and mind.

The various elements, components, entities and parameters that come into play in Vastushastra associated ceremonies can be tabulated as follows:

Table 7.3: Elements of Vedic Origin in Vastushastra Ceremonies

Panch-Maha-Bhutas (Five Gross Elements)	*Prithvi* (Earth), *Aap* (Water), *Tej* (Fire), *Vayu* (Air), *Akash* (Ether)
Tanmatras (Five Subtle Elements)	*Gandha* (Smell), *Rasa* (Taste), *Rupa* (Form), *Sparsha* (Touch), *Shabda* (Sound)
Gunas (Qualities & Evolutionary Powers)	*Sattva* (Illumination), *Rajas* (Activity), *Tamas* (Dormancy) form *Mahat* (Cosmic Intellect). *Ahamkara* (Ego), *Buddhi* (Intellect), *Manas* (Mind) form *Chitta* (Consciousness)
Jnanendriyas (Five Organs of Perception)	Ear, Nose, Tongue, Eye, Skin
Karmendriyas (Five Senses of Action)	Legs, Arms, Speech, Excretory Organs, Reproductive Organs.

8

CONCLUDING REMARKS

The Vastushastra concepts presented in this book are consistent with the perceptions in Yogshastra, Astrology and Ayurveda. Some readers may consider these ideas as appearing to be far-fetched from the point of view of scientific logic as imbibed by the present-day scientific community. Since the effects of application of certain Vastushastra principles are well-documented, it is but natural to look for the causes in modern scientific concepts. But certain areas in science, especially modern theoretical physics, are yet in an evolutionary stage. The scientific logic is not complete without total comprehension of Grand Unification Theory, Quark Theory, Super-string Theory which are not fully developed. But consideration given to deficiencies in these theories must also be offered to some drawbacks observed in logical explanation of Vastushastra principles. A thought process cannot be termed unscientific, just because it is beyond the grasp of modern science.

One of the interesting developments in theoretical modern physics is a theorem postulated by Dr J.S.Bell of C.E.R.N Laboratories at Zurich which indicates that either the statistical predictions of quantum theory or the principles of local causes is false and that the macroscopic responses are not independent of faraway causes. Bell's theorem says that there is no such thing as 'separate parts', and all of the parts of the universe at a deep and fundamental level are connected in an intimate and immediate way. As Gary Zukav in *Dancing Wu-Li Masters* puts it, " In short, Bell's theorem and the enlightened view of unity are compatible." In a way this Bell's theorem endorses the 'cosmic harmony and unity' concept of Vastushastra.

The self-professed 'rationalists' dismiss the Vastushastra related subjects like Astrology, Yogshastra, Five Elements, Shapes, Colours, Numerology, Cosmic Energy, Bio-electromagnetic Effects as unscientific. As such, it is a challenge for dedicated scientists and scholars to come forward with the correct picture, rather than ignoring the related ideas without any logical verification. The main aim of this book is to evaluate Vastushastra in terms of established scientific ideas, so that principles enunciated in Vastushastra find wider application in all walks of life.

Darshanshastra says that, "when the mind unfolds like sunlight, the image that is created internally in the conscious is knowledge, the understanding, and the sensitivity." There is a profound truth in this far-reaching definition of *perception.*

Darshanshastra analyses and interprets the process of hearing in a totally different manner as compared to the established theories. It says that the ear continuously emits micro-reference waves, like a radar. When these waves interact with the sound waves from an external source, the sound is noted as melodious if the interaction is harmonious and as incoherent noise otherwise. Many scientists are either not aware of this theory or dismiss it altogether. But this *Darshanic* concept received wider acceptance when scientist Hugo Zucarelli in 1983, based on experimental recordings of Hero Wit wherein emission of continuous sound waves in the range 1 - 2 kHz from a healthy human ear were detected, put forward a new hypothesis that the ear sends an outgoing reference wave which interacts with the incoming waves to produce an acoustic hologram in the brain. Here, a theory dismissed as unscientific was proved as valid by some ingenuous experimental techniques.

With a little stimulation to the brain and some broadminded thinking, it is possible to detect a common thread running through apparently dissimilar entities and processes derived from vastly different fields encompassing Vastushastra, Astrology, Yogashastra, Ayurveda, Music, Numerology, etc.

We end this narration by quoting a paragraph from an article by the internationally known eminent scientist Prof. E.C.G.Sudarshan:

At present most scientists are educated in Western objective methods. Therefore, many scientists are deeply suspicious of anything that is not based on science. In many cases, the scientist becomes aware of other dimensions and subjective experiences. Then he isolates them as personal experiences, while he keeps science as public. But if he is not able to reconcile some experiences within a system, he could enlarge the system of ideas by borrowing from Darshanshastras. The world is continually growing and we should welcome ideas from other sources. In this process of integrating science and Darshanshastras, there are bound to be conflicts. But we should have the right perception to resolve these minor differences and accept the complementarity of the two approaches.

Summing up

The inanimate world, the plant kingdom, the animal kingdom, and then the human being are but progressive states of evolution of the one and the same element. The culture inherited by us aims at a healthy life which is defined by coherent and harmonious interaction of all these states. On its part, Vastushastra gives fruition to these ideas by using different entities like soil, stone, mortar, water, fire and direction to provide a harmonically balanced living environment for the human beings.

On the face of it, blind faith and metaphysics seem to govern the practice of Vastushastra. Deep and serious thinking reveals that the logic and the reasoning of Vastushastra is not only remarkable, but its symbolism withstands the scrutiny of modern science. It is to be noted that the mathematical principles attributed to Archimedes and Pythagoras can be traced to ancient scriptures written well before the era of these mathematicians. Similarly, the microscopic effects documented in Vastushastra reflect many of the modern concepts from the fields of particle physics, radiation, electromagnetism, bio-physics, bio-chemistry and gravitation. Throughout the book we have tried to establish this correlation through regression analysis of the effects forecast by Vastushastra and drawing of inferences based on scientific concepts.

There may be a few inadvertent errors and mistakes as regards symbolic similarity and presentation of modern scientific concepts in this writing, which we earnestly hope will be modified or rectified by scholars and scientists committed to incisive and objective thinking. Even if a few readers are prompted or inspired to look at Vastushastra from a scientific point of view, it would be a major gain for this field.

In the fields of electricity and magnetism, rapid progress* could be achieved once the basic principles were understood. In the same way, application of Vastushastra can cover wider areas of life if efforts are made to understand its principles.

It is matter of time before the mystic science of Vastushastra is decoded and its all encompassing principles are found to reflect the insights of natural sciences.

---

* Prof. E.C.Cullwick says : "The known facts of electricity and magnetism form an exact and coherent body of knowledge of surprising beauty and symmetry, and unravelling of this beauty by patient thought and experiment forms one of the most fascinating stories of all times. From a small and disjointed beginning, from lodestone and amber, this most incorporeal of nature's-secrets gradually capitulated to the restless mind of man until at last the knowledge handed on by Oersted and Faraday, by Ampere and Maxwell bids fair to embrace the whole of physical universe."

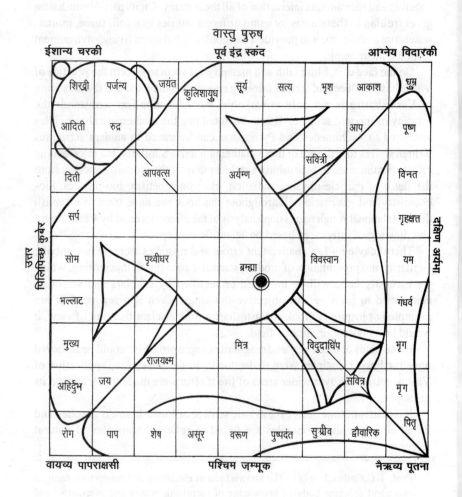

वास्तु पुरुष

ईशान्य चरकी				पूर्व इंद्र स्कंद			आग्नेय विदारकी
शिखी	पर्जन्य	जयंत	कुलिशायुध	सूर्य	सत्य	भृश	आकाश	धूम्र
आदिती	रुद्र					आप		पूष्ण
दिती		आपवत्स		अर्यम्ण	सवित्री		विनत
सर्प							गृह्क्षत
सोम		पृथ्वीधर		ब्रम्हा	विवस्वान		यम
भल्लाट							गंधर्व
मुख्य		राजयक्ष्म		मित्र	विदुदारिषप		भृग
अहिर्दुभ	जय					सवित्र	मृग
							पितृ
रोग	पाप	शेष	असूर	वरुण	पुष्पदंत	सुग्रीव	द्वौवारिक

उत्तर मिलिपिक्क कुबेर

दक्षिण अर्यम्ना

वायव्य पापराक्षसी   पश्चिम जम्मूक   नैऋव्य पूतना

Vastu Purush

BIBLIOGRAPHY

Ananda Shri : *Yoga, Harmony of Body & Mind* (Orient Paperbacks, New Delhi, 1993)

Birla Institute of Scientific Research: *Social Forestry in India* (Radiant Publishers, New Delhi, 1984)

Biswas, S.K. et al (ed.) : *Cosmic Perspectives* (Cambridge University Press, Cambridge, U.K., 1989)

Cheiro : *Cheiro's Book of Numbers* (Arrow Books Limited, London, 1986)

Chopra, Dr. Deepak : *Quantum Healing*

Feynman, Richard D.: *Surely You're Joking, Mr Feynman* (Bantam Books, New York, 1988)

Frish S.E.: *Problems of Wave Optics* (Mir Publishers, Moscow, 1973)

Gambhiranand Swami : *Eight Upanishads - Vol. II* (Advaita Ashrama, Calcutta, 1992)

Gardner, Martin: *The Ambidextrous Universe* (Penguin Books Ltd., Middlesex, England, 1979)

— (ed.) : *Great Essays in Science* (Washington Square Press, New York, 1970)

Ginzburg, V.L.: *Key Problems : Physics & Astronomy* (Mir Publishers, Moscow, 1978)

Hewish, A. : *Physics of the Universe* (Council of Scientific & Industrial Research, New Delhi, 1994)

Iyengar B.K.S.: *Light on Pranayama* (Harper Collins Publ. India Pvt Ltd., New Delhi, 1996)

Lip, Evelyn: *Feng-Shui for the Home* (Times Books International, Singapore, 1995)

Laithwaite, Eric: *An Inventor in the Garden of Eden* (Cambridge University Press, Cambridge, U.K.)

F.David Peat : *Superstrings and the Search for Theory of Everything* (Abacus, London, 1992)

Parnov E.I. : *At the Crossroads of Infinities* (Mir Publishers, Moscow, 1971)

Schul Bill, Petit (Ed) : *The Secret Powers of Pyramids* (Random House Inc., New York,1983)

Tarasov L.: *This Amazingly Symmetrical World* (Mir Publishers, Moscow, 1986)

Zukav Gary : *The Dancing Wu Li Masters* (Bantam Books, New York, 1980)

For Further Reading

Books on Vastushastra in Sanskrit/Hindi/Tamil/Translated Versions

1. *Vastu Raj Vallabh* - Anup Mishra
2. *Vastu Muktavali* - Radharaman Pande
3. *Vastu Ratnakosh* - Jaivijay Muni
4. *Samrangan Sutradhar* - Bhojraj / Ganapati Shastri
5. *Mayamatam* - Translated by Bruno Dagenes
6. *Shilpa Ratnakosh* - Betina Boumer, Rajendraprasad Das
7. *Vishwa Karma Prakash* (North India) - Comprehensive text on Vastu
8. *Vastu Vidya* (North India) - General commentry on Vastu techniques
9. *Maana Saara* (South India) - Five thousand *shlokas* on Vastushastra
10. *Maya Saar* (South India) - Extensive treatment of Vastu concepts

Books on Hindu Philosophy (English / Indian Languages)

1. *World Vedic Heritage* - P.N. Oke
2. *Studies in Indian Philosophy* - Prof. R.D. Ranade
3. *Introduction to Every Human is Hindu* - B.R.Mudholkar
4. *Shiv Vahi* - Dr. Shiv Muni
5. *Shiv Swarodaya Shastra*
6. *Sense Perception for Science and Sastras* - Sri Sharada Trust, Shringeri
7. *Agni Sampada* - S.K.Kulkarni
8. *Achuk Nidan* - Udhav Vishnu Ruikar
9. *Taitireya Upanishad*

General References

1. *Encyclopedia Britannica*
2. *Oxford World Atlas*
3. *The World Book of Encyclopedia*

P-105 - Veda.

Mandelas / science IONA

{
CD
video / CD-Rom

book on Dharma

= blessing

3 BODIES :- mantras

_____

waves → sound → light →
(see) perception → Intelligence